STRAIGHT FROM THE ADMISSIONS OFFICE

INSIDER STRATEGIES FOR COLLEGE APPLICATIONS

DR. JOHN DURANTE

WWW.COLLEGEADMISSIONSTALK.COM

JOIN MY EMAIL LIST

Scan this QR code to stay updated with more insights and resources!

CONTENTS

Dedication	xi
Introduction	xiii
1. VIRTUAL COLLEGE FAIR	1
2. OVERVIEW OF THE HIGHER EDUCATION LANDSCAPE	3
3. FINDING THE RIGHT FIT—MAKING A BALANCED COLLEGE LIST	7
4. QUALITIES OF A BALANCED COLLEGE LIST	13
5. THE COMPONENTS OF A COLLEGE APPLICATION	35
6. THE TRANSCRIPT	37
7. EXTRACURRICULAR ACTIVITIES	47
8. STANDARDIZED TESTS	52
9. THE PERSONAL STATEMENT	60
10. SUPPLEMENTAL ESSAYS	70
11. LETTERS OF RECOMMENDATION	76
12. DEMONSTRATING YOUR INTEREST	80
13. APPLICATION TYPES	90
The Common Application	90
The University of California	93
The State University of New York	95
The Coalition Application	96
Individual applications	97
14. APPLICATION DEADLINES	98
Early Decision (ED) 1	99
Early Decision (ED) 2	100
Early Action (EA)	100
Restrictive Early Action (REA) or Single Choice Early Action (SCEA)	101
Regular Decision	101
Rolling Admissions	102
15. THE ROLE OF A COLLEGE ADMISSIONS OFFICIAL	103
16. COLLEGE ADMISSIONS INTERVIEWS	108
17. APPLICATION RESPONSES	116
Acceptance	116
Rejection	117

Waitlisted	119
Deferred	122
Financial aid award	123
18. THE TEN MOST COMMON TYPES OF FOUR-YEAR COLLEGES AND UNIVERSITIES	124
The Big 10	124
Land-grant universities	125
Liberal arts colleges	126
The Ivy League	128
Tech schools	129
Single-sex schools	130
Religious-affiliated schools	131
The HBCU System	132
Service academies	133
Art colleges	134
19. INTERNATIONAL APPLICANTS	136
20. FOR-PROFIT HIGHER EDUCATION	142
21. ASSESSING YOUR APPLICATION PROFILE	147
22. THE THINGS THAT ARE OUT OF YOUR HANDS	153
Legacy admissions	154
Quotas	159
Athletics and Performing Arts	159
Yield rates	160
Family income	163
23. FINANCIAL AID - HOW TO AFFORD COLLEGE	164
24. A WORD ABOUT TWO-YEAR COLLEGES	170
25. FINAL ADVICE	172
Join My Email List	177
Additional Resources	179
Podcast Episodes	181
About the Author	191

Copyright © 2024 by John Durante

All rights reserved.

No part of this publication may be reproduced, distributed, or transmitted in any form or by any means, including photocopying, recording, or other electronic or mechanical methods, without the prior written permission of the publisher, except as permitted by U.S. copyright law. For permission requests, contact the author at

john@collegeadmissionstalk.com

Editing, Cover Design, and Interior Design: Jason Morgan of Plotworks Publishing

ISBN (print): 979-8-9919542-0-4

ISBN (electronic): 979-8-9919542-1-1

DEDICATION

I dedicate this book to my parents, Angelo and Felicia Durante, who left their homeland of Italy to come to the United States in search of a better life for our family. Thanks to their love, courage, and effort, I am proud to be a first-generation college student. It is an honor to carry on their legacy by helping others navigate their own college journeys. My work pales in comparison to the sacrifices they made in leaving everything behind to provide more opportunities for their family, and for that I am forever grateful. I love you, Mom and Dad.

I also dedicate this book to my wife Roseanne, and daughters Alyssa and Julianna. Thank you for helping me to see the college admissions process from the perspective of a parent, which helped me to develop such a concept to help other students, parents and school counselors. Your unwavering support, commitment and encouragement throughout inspired me to continue with this work. Without your love and understanding, I wouldn't be able to dedicate so much time to helping others. I love you and know how blessed I am to have you.

Lastly, I want to extend my heartfelt thanks to the admissions professionals who have generously shared their time and expertise on *The College Admissions Process Podcast*. Your openness and willingness to work with me have provided listeners with a deeper understanding of the college admissions process, and your insights have been invaluable to this work.

INTRODUCTION

While you know me as a podcast host, I've been working at Syosset High School, in Syosset, New York, for over 30 years. I started as a teacher of world languages, and have been the principal since 2010.

But that wasn't what led me to starting *The College Admissions Process Podcast*. It was something different.

During the covid-19 pandemic in 2020 and 2021, I became a big fan of podcasts. Obviously, we all had a lot more time on our hands during that time, and I loved the on-demand nature of the medium. Whether I was taking a walk, exercising, or doing dishes, I could tune into anything anywhere basically any time. Because I am a huge soccer fan, referee, and coach, I listened to *Coaching Soccer Weekly* and *Modern Soccer Coach*. I came to love the information available in an audio format, which suits my style of learning by listening. Soon I began to think about launching a podcast of my own. I enjoy helping people and am happy when I am able to do so. When I was much younger, I used to be a DJ, so this is something that is in my blood.

Around that time, I was actively involved in helping my two daughters navigate the college application process, experiencing it not as a principal, but as a parent who, like so many, was deeply invested in their futures. For my youngest daughter, who had an Individualized Education Plan (IEP) in high school, this journey presented unique challenges. While school had always been more difficult for her, I was determined to advocate for her and find a college that would be a supportive and nurturing environment. This experience gave me a firsthand understanding of the pressures and uncertainties that many families face, and it reinforced my commitment to finding the right fit for her, where she could truly thrive.

I began talking with college admissions representatives. They told me that my direct questions were refreshing. Some of the reps I spoke to said that many people were skeptical about reaching out to them. Many of the applicants and their families didn't even know what questions to ask. After all, there is so much fear about the process, particularly among the families of first-generation college students. I didn't feel that type of fear, and you really shouldn't either—especially not after reading this book.

That's when it hit me. I decided that I would start asking those questions in public. I would ask them on a podcast, like the ones that I enjoyed during the pandemic.

But I wanted to do a podcast that, frankly, was going to last. The sad fact is that the majority of podcasts fail very quickly. Most of the hosts don't understand how much work goes into recording and editing a podcast, especially if you're a one-man show, like I am.

So, I made a couple of promises to myself. One, I was going to put the time and energy into the project to do it right. Two, I would do something that was going to truly help people.

I knew early that my podcast episodes would be interview style, each one with a different college admissions representative who would provide insights and tips to students (and their parents) who are getting ready to apply for college. Based on the nature of my interview style podcast episodes, and knowing that I would be speaking to representatives outside of my home state of New York, I researched the best ways to record podcast episodes remotely. I came across a platform called riverside.fm, which helps podcasters do all of that and so much more from the comfort of a laptop computer. The quality of their product is excellent, and I have never left their side. I purchased a USB microphone and headset package for podcasters, and my studio was born. I've since upgraded the microphone, but that's still pretty much what my podcast studio consists of today, years later.

I started with the reps who I'd known from my own daughters' college searches. But they weren't the only ones. I politely approached several others, and I was surprised at how many were willing to be interviewed. Many college admissions representatives have been very good to me on this journey.

One by one, they came on my show and had interesting conversations with me about their schools, and all the great things their programs offer. They have come from across the spectrum of higher education, from Big Ten universities to the Ivy League to tech schools. Through them, the podcast provides a diverse range of perspectives and approaches to the college admissions process, while revealing nuances between institutions. My conversations with these guests have covered topics such as standardized tests, college essays, visiting schools and how to approach the overall application.

Most importantly, they were happy to give insights into their application review process, straight from the admissions representatives who are part of the team that ultimately makes the decisions. This information really resonated with a lot of listeners. I think both the reps and the applicants were feeling the same thing that I was: that there was a communications gap. Admissions officials are sometimes viewed as all powerful deities by the applicants and their families. It shouldn't work like that. I don't believe that fear, or that communication gap, is healthy. We're all just people, and the sooner we cross these self-imposed barriers the better.

The podcast seems to have struck a chord. As of this writing, I've recorded more than 250 episodes, all available on my website (www.collegeadmissionstalk.com). I release episodes weekly. So far, I've literally had representatives from every corner of the United States and beyond. The number of episode downloads has exceeded my expectations, which is why I continue to do this work. Knowing that I am helping students and their families motivates me.

It didn't take long for me to recognize some patterns in their responses. College admissions representatives have told me repeatedly that they really want to admit each and every applicant. They tell me that paying for college has become an ever-more urgent problem, as the sticker price for college keeps escalating. They're just as worried about it as the applicants' parents are. Mostly, however, they tell me that they take a "holistic" approach to application review. This means that they look at all the elements of the college application—at the school transcript, at the personal statement and supplementary essays, at the extracurricular activities, at the letters of recommendation.

But none of these elements is a make-or-break. There's no single thing that guarantees admission. The term *holistic* refers to the interconnectedness of every element of a system, and so it is with college applications too.

It's no joke. You'll hear this term *holistic*, or something like it, in just about every single episode of my podcast. To students and parents, what that means is that you have to be very mindful to understand how each part of the application package has to build upon the next. You have to show the best essence of yourself as a candidate, and you have to do all of that without repeating information.

A college application is essentially a marketing strategy. In this case, though, you are both the product and the one who is marketing it.

I like to say that there's not just one school for every student. In fact, there's more than one school for every student. But it's equally important to understand that not every school is for every student. It's a match to be made, not a race to be won.

Hence the importance of not worrying about where your mom and dad went to college, or where your older brother or sister is going to college. Hence the importance of not worrying about which sticker your parents get to put on the back of the family car. Hence the importance of not worrying about where your friends are going to go to college.

Lastly, it's very important to do your research. Start early! The fact that you're reading or listening to this book puts you miles ahead of the competition. The other good news is that today, whether through podcasts, virtual meetings, or websites, there is an abundance of resources online, far more than I ever had when I was younger. It's really important to take advantage of all of them, especially visiting campus. That's key. I know that it's tough for some people, especially if you're interested in schools thousands of miles away, on the other side of the country. Still, if you can't visit campus before you apply, you owe it to yourself to visit before you matriculate.

By hosting the College Admissions Process podcast, I've learned so much about college admissions. I have loved sharing it all with you, whether you are an applicant or a family member. Though I didn't realize it at first, these episodes have also served as a valuable tool for school counselors as they guide students through the application process.

Thank you for joining me on this journey. It is my hope that the advice and insights shared will empower you to navigate the college admissions process with confidence, success, and a lot more clarity. Should you have any questions or feedback for me, please don't hesitate to email me at: john@collegeadmissionstalk.com

Now, please keep reading to find out more.

CHAPTER 1
VIRTUAL COLLEGE FAIR

THE PURPOSE of the podcast and this review of the first 250 episodes is to serve students (and parents) going through the college admissions process by providing insights and advice straight from the people who ultimately make the decisions: the college admissions representatives.

This book serves not only as a summary of the most important lessons learned over the first 250 episodes, but it provides important resources in the form of QR codes and links. This is designed to foster an interactive experience for its readers. Many of the links you can follow via QR codes will be updated as new episodes and resources become available. For a comprehensive understanding of the many aspects of the college admissions process, I suggest using this book in conjunction with the podcast episodes.

The first of these resources is the alphabetical list of schools with whom I interviewed an admissions representative, along with other related episodes, to give you insights and advice straight from the admissions offices. Once you access the alphabetical list, click on the name of the school to access the audio file of the related podcast episode. When you visit campus or a college fair, you will be equipped with the ability to ask better follow-up questions after hearing each of the episodes, based on your own interests, needs, or concerns.

In short, the alphabetical list serves as an on-demand college fair where you can listen to the conversations at your leisure, as often and whenever you wish, without being rushed or interrupted by others waiting for their turn, as is the case oftentimes on campus or at a college fair.

Scan the following QR code, and create a shortcut to the link, as it is updated weekly as new episodes become available:

CHAPTER 2
OVERVIEW OF THE HIGHER EDUCATION LANDSCAPE

IN THE UNITED STATES, post-secondary education begins after high school graduation. Students have three options for post-secondary education:

- vocational training (typically one or two years, designed for immediate employment in a trade)
- a 2-year associate's degree (typically granted by community colleges)
- A 4-year bachelor's degree (also called an undergraduate degree)

All post-secondary institutions are called either *colleges* or *universities*, and the words are often used interchangeably. Colleges offer undergraduate-level programs that lead to both associate and bachelor's degrees, while universities offer both undergraduate and graduate programs that lead to bachelor's degrees and graduate degrees. What sometimes creates confusion is the fact that a university is technically a collection of colleges, such as the College of Engineering or College of Nursing. But a college can also stand completely on its own, such as Oberlin College (Episode 217).

The U.S. federal government doesn't operate any colleges or

universities. However, the governments of all 50 states and territories definitely do: they run all state university systems such as the University of Michigan or Arizona State University. But sometimes that can be confusing too, because there are some universities containing the names of states that are nonetheless private schools. For instance, the University of Pennsylvania (episode 166) is a private school, not a public one.

What nobody is debating is the sheer size of our system of higher education. In 2020, the United States had 5916 post-secondary schools, according to the National Center for Education Statistics. Of those, roughly even numbers were public (1892) and private (1754), and the remainder were for-profit (2270).

This system of higher education is one of the jewels of the United States. It is a major reason that millions of immigrants are drawn to our shores, year after year, decade after decade. These institutions, which are less plentiful elsewhere, hold the promise of better lives for them and for their children.

For undergraduate degrees, the three most common types of degrees are

- BA (Bachelor of Arts) - includes the liberal arts and social sciences
- BS (Bachelor of Science) - includes all STEM fields
- BFA (Bachelor of Fine Arts) - includes the creative arts

There are many others, but those are by far the most common.

Remember, since the university system isn't regulated by the federal government, there isn't any federal Department of Certification for colleges and universities. Instead, there is a private accreditation system made of six regional accreditation groups that regulate the private and public nonprofit colleges. (There is a separate national system of accreditation for for-profit universities.) There are separate accreditation programs for specific programs as well—engineering, for example.

All of this is to say that you want to go to an accredited college or university. That should be a goal. Accredited colleges and universities tend to offer a higher quality of education. They are easier to transfer credits from if transferring becomes an option. Plus, future employers usually look at the school you graduated from, and a diploma from an accredited school will say better things about you than a diploma from an unaccredited school.

Colleges and universities typically run on the semester system, though a few operate on quarters and even trimesters. Lynn University offers a trimester system in which students take fewer courses each term, as a way to help them become more focused on their courses while helping them to succeed academically. For more details about their unique structure, listen to podcast Episode 183. A handful of private schools offer a so-called "J-term", which is a short winter session of 2 to 4 weeks. Occurring in January, it is a time for students to pursue a single challenging class, or a special project. Carleton College (Episode 91) is one such example.

Class sizes depend on the school and the major. For required classes at larger public universities, freshmen and sophomores will often find themselves in lecture halls of 200 people. At those same universities, juniors and seniors will often find themselves in smaller classes of 20 for advanced coursework in their major. At private colleges, students may never find themselves in classes with more than 15 students.

Outside of pass-fail classes, most classes are measured in academic credits. Some classes are worth 3 credits; others can be worth 5. That number usually corresponds with the number of weekly hours that a student will spend in lecture or in lab for that class. To graduate, students typically need to complete 120 credits total, with a predetermined number of those credits within their majors. A major usually requires anywhere between 30 and 50 credits, while a minor requires only 18 to 30. A minor is useful insofar as it allows you to explore fields outside your major, and it could help when seeking your first job after college.

A bachelor's degree has been a ticket into the middle class for decades, but there are signs that changes are coming. In the four years from 2019 to 2023, enrollment in higher education fell by 7.5 percent. A major demographic change—the shrinking of the number of young people—doesn't bode well either. Because of the baby bust of 2009, the overall enrollment between 2024 and 2029 is projected to decline by 9 percent.

The cost of higher education is a major concern, and wise university presidents recognize that they can't keep raising tuition costs forever. They need to find alternate sources of revenue. This is one of the biggest challenges facing the survival of some of the colleges lower down on the food chain. It may be that successful institutions of higher education create hybrid models of education that involve skills training, online classes mixed with in-person education, and even offering non-degree credentials. About 1 in 3 college students never complete their degree, and schools may try to find ways to keep these students enrolled. The traditional paper-based university would be well-advised to create simple enrollment and administrative systems, using modern cloud-based functions, that can help younger digital natives feel at home.

But that's enough of the staring into the crystal ball. This book exists to help you right here, right now. With that said, let's get into how to make a college list.

CHAPTER 3
FINDING THE RIGHT FIT—MAKING A BALANCED COLLEGE LIST

ONE OF THE questions that I typically ask my guests on the podcast is, "What is it about your school that makes it so appealing, for so many students to want to apply and ultimately attend?" The admissions representatives usually touch upon items such as their location, academic and extracurricular offerings, internship and study abroad opportunities, along with research accessibility just to name a few.

What I believe is most important to recognize is that just because a school may receive over 50,000 applications, or perhaps you've seen it consistently listed as a top 20 school in the country, it doesn't mean that it is the right fit for you. The college admissions process is very personal, and taking a deep dive into what you are looking for in a college experience is very important to help you find the school that you will be happy with over the course of your college years.

If a school is consistently listed in the top 20 on all the ranking lists, but it is located in an urban environment when you're looking for a school in a rural area, that school is not for you. If a school is a five-hour airplane ride from your home, and you come to realize that you want to be within a two-hour car ride, that school is not for you. Regardless of its academic reputation, which of your friends is applying to that school, and its placement on the ranking lists, if the school doesn't meet the criteria that you identify as important to you, then you should not apply. Schools take a lot of time and care to select those who will be admitted, you should do the same and more as part of your college search.

When researching a school, keep in mind that for every student there are a multitude of schools that are the right fit for them. Equally as important is to remember that not every school is right for every student, and taking the time to research, reflect and discover what you want in a college education is an essential part of the overall process, as it may save you a lot of time and money later. The college search process is in fact about you as an individual, not about where your friends want to attend college. Don't take for granted what you are looking for in a college education and understand that even the most popular schools in the country are not the right "fit" for everyone.

There are many items that schools can use to entice potential students to attend. Academic programs, majors and minors, study abroad opportunities, the presence of a Greek system, etc. Geographic location, campus size, climate and whether they can guarantee housing for all four years of your undergraduate education, include some of the items that a college or university has less control over. So, do not underestimate the importance of reflecting on these questions, while coming up with your own questions too, based on what is important to you. There are no right or wrong answers. Each of us are unique in our own personalities, needs, interests, and intended course of study. So, be true to yourself and what you are seeking in a college education, which will surely steer you towards making the right decisions about where to apply.

———

Here are some criteria that you should consider while assembling a college list:

- *Do I want to live at home, or do I want to go away to college? In other words, am I interested in commuting or living on campus?*

- *Am I fine with attending a school which requires an airplane ride, or do I want to go to a school within driving distance from my home? What is the maximum distance I am willing to travel by plane or car?*
- *Would I be more successful at a larger university that may offer more options while including lecture-hall style classes? Or do I prefer a smaller college that generally provides a more intimate feel and more professor interaction?*
- *Do I want to be in an urban, suburban, or rural environment? Is the surrounding area off-campus important to me in terms of safety, internship opportunities, shopping, restaurants, recreational activities, or other things?*
- *Does the climate where my school is located matter to me? Do I study better in hot weather or cold weather? Which one will make me happier?*
- *Have I selected my major and am applying to schools that offer a competitive program in my chosen coursework? Or am I undecided and want to attend a school that offers many options to students who are undecided?*
- *What if I had an IEP or 504 Plan while in high school? Does the college I am applying to offer support and resources to help me continue to be successful?*
- *Is joining a sorority or fraternity important to me? If so, do the schools I am applying to offer this opportunity?*
- *Am I interested in studying abroad? If so, where?*
- *Is cost a factor? If so, are private schools, which are generally more expensive, an option for me? Do I need to find a job while on campus, and does the school offer a work study program?*

Using this list, I would encourage you to make a checklist with every quality that you're looking for in a college. Color code the qualities as to their importance to you: green is mandatory, yellow is preferred, red is unimportant.

However, it is vital that you also recognize that there is probably not going to be a single school that satisfies every box on your wish list. That's why color coding is important. It will show you what you are willing to bend on, and doing so can open up an abundance of new possibilities for you.

Let's look at a case study. Emily lives in a suburb of Chicago. She is a straight-A student with a lot of interesting extracurricular activities, including varsity golf and volunteering for a local political campaign. She assembles a list of qualities for her college that looks like this:

- Live on campus
- Four-hour driving distance or less
- Small college (I like to talk in class)
- Urban/rural environment doesn't matter
- Cold weather, yes
- Politics major, for now
- No Greek system, never
- Study abroad, definitely
- Not sure about cost

You can see from this list that Emily is limiting herself to small colleges within a four-hour drive from Chicago. Lucky for her, there's one school that would fit every part of her checklist: Kalamazoo College, in Kalamazoo, Michigan. So that would be a definite number one.

However, if she became more flexible about the no-Greek-life requirement, she could also apply to Beloit College (in Wisconsin) and Northwestern University (Episode 257) in Evanston, a suburb of Chicago. Those schools have everything she's looking for, but they also include a moderate-sized fraternity and sorority scene. If she expanded her preferred geographic radius, she could also add Macalester College (Episode 190) in Minneapolis, Minnesota, or Creighton University in Omaha, Nebraska.

Because she's a politics major for now, she'll want to select a college that makes it easy to switch majors, if she changes her mind. Fortunately, at most schools, that is easy to do for liberal arts majors. Likewise, most schools have study-abroad programs now, but Kalamazoo College goes one step further. There, almost all students study abroad during junior year.

So, you should make a firm checklist to see if any school ticks all your boxes. Once you've done that, try bending on one or two of your non-negotiables, and see what other institutions you might catch in your net.

———

How many schools should you apply to? That answer is different for everyone. Some students are comfortable only applying to three schools; others decide they need to apply to 20 to sleep well at night. A good rule of thumb, whatever you choose, is to have at least two safety schools, at least two target schools, and at least two reach schools.

What do those terms mean? Here are the definitions:

- **Safety school**: A college or university that is almost guaranteed to accept you. This is primarily determined by your GPA, but it's not the only ingredient. Most commonly, a safety school is a large public school, such as Arizona State University (Episode 122).
- **Target school**: A college or university that may or may not accept you. At this institution, you fall into the middle range of typical students, both in GPA and standardized tests. The majority of the schools you apply to should be of this type.
- **Reach school**: A college or university that is almost guaranteed to reject you. This includes any school with a sub-15 percent acceptance rate. That includes all Ivy League schools, Ivy League-plus schools, West Point, and others.

Here is what a poorly balanced school list looks like:

Safety: 0
Target: 2
Reach: 8

This person seems like that overly ambitious, often unrealistic guy in your class who has a shortage of common sense. Everyone knows someone like that. This person is asking for trouble, and may not end up attending college at all when all his reach schools reject him as do (with a touch of additional bad luck) both target schools. If you know someone like this, try to talk some sense to him.

Listen to what Tim Fields, senior associate dean of undergraduate admissions at Emory University (Episode 211), told me: "There are over 4000 colleges and universities in this country, and 2000 offer bachelor's degrees. For whatever reason, there is an emphasis on about 100 of those schools. And too many times people get caught up in specific institutions that have very low admit rates and are wondering why there is so much pressure in this process. There is not a lot of pressure in this process. It only comes if you limit yourself to these schools that everyone is applying to."

Here's another type of poorly balanced list:

Safety: 5
Target: 1
Reach: 0

This person probably suffers from lack of self-esteem. This person may doubt herself severely, so much that she does not believe that she could be accepted at a target school, where her GPA and standardized test scores plant her firmly in the middle range of acceptances. While this applicant will end up safely going to college, it will be at a school with a lesser reputation, lesser facilities, and fewer opportunities. If you know someone like this, try to talk sense to her too.

Instead, let's look at what a well-balanced school list looks like:

Safety: 2
Target: 6
Reach: 2

This student is prudent and practical. Most applicants end up going to a target school, so making that the biggest group of the list is wise. This person has common sense and should do well in the college admissions process.

CHAPTER 4
QUALITIES OF A BALANCED COLLEGE LIST

CHOOSING a school to apply to is a lot like buying a car. It's a big-ticket item that you don't do very often. Without someone to serve as a guide, you could make an error that will make the next several years of your life more difficult or more unhappy than they need to be.

In the previous chapter, I provided a list of qualities that you need to consider when assembling your college list. Those qualities are so important that I'd like to address them in a bit more length.

Engaging in a bit of self-reflection right now, before you begin your college journey, will avoid many problems along the way. People who don't consider these questions will sometimes end up needing to transfer to a different school. While that isn't the end of the world, transferring between four-year universities also isn't something you should really seek out either. Credits sometimes don't transfer easily, and the entire bachelor's degree could become more expensive and longer than it needs to be.

Let's take a look at each of them in turn.

―――

Do I want to live at home, or do I want to go away to college? In other words, am I interested in commuting or living on campus?

· · ·

Knowing the answer to this question will obviously help you select schools to apply to that will fit your geographic needs. If you have decided to stay home for college, and many students do, you will need to consider what your commute will look like and whether you are driving or taking public transportation if available.

Many students remain undecided throughout the application process, and therefore apply to schools that are both close to home, and away. Doing so gives you and your family more time to visit schools and really get a sense of what is the right fit for you. Once you start receiving acceptances from schools, hopefully you have been doing your research, and are better prepared to make your final decision.

Let's look at the benefits of living at home:

- **Cost**. For many, cost is a major consideration, as living at home will often save you the cost of room and board, which can be very expensive. Many students often stay local by going to community college for two years, then transferring later to a full four-year university for the last two years of undergraduate. This is a very common money-saving technique in California, for instance, which has a strong community college system. For example, Orange Coast College (Episode 115) is a public community college and part of the California College System. At the very least, commuting to a public school will give you the advantage of in-state tuition.
- **A support network**. Living at home does offer familiarity, and for people who have anxiety or uncertainty about living on their own, this might be the best option. It can reduce stress, eliminate homesickness, and offer the student more flexibility regarding the decision to move out. The covid-19 pandemic has had a powerful effect on young people's perspectives on life, and this option is no longer seen as undesirable as it once was. Young people do actually enjoy

staying home much more than they did before. This may also be the better option for people with health issues or learning disabilities.

The drawbacks of living at home:

- **Commuting is a hassle.** When your house is twenty miles from campus, and you barely have enough money to buy gasoline for the week, social events suddenly seem less important. Driving all the way back to campus just for a Saturday movie night that may not draw more than ten people might not seem worth it. This is a hazard faced by commuter schools everywhere: they tend to turn into ghost towns on the weekends.
- **Limited socializing with classmates.** People often carry college friends with them all the way through life, and it's flat out easier to meet your classmates when you are walking around campus seven days a week, or (especially) living in the dorms. As a result, people living off campus miss out on building key relationships that will benefit them later in life.

If you are certain that you want to go away for college, the remaining questions will help you narrow your search in terms of what is important to you and where you should apply.

Am I fine with attending a school which requires an airplane ride, or do I want to go to a school within driving distance from my home? What is the maximum distance I am willing to travel by plane or car?

This is another important question that should be reviewed with your family, since airplane travel will certainly add to your cost of attending. If you are accustomed to being away for long periods of time from your family, perhaps being an airplane ride away is simply not a big deal for you.

However, if this is your first time on your own, even though you may think you want to be as far away as possible, you should consider the realities of being an airplane ride from home. If there is a family gathering for someone's birthday, including your own, it's not as simple to get together with the family, as opposed to being a car ride away from home. If you get sick, and want to be close to family, this is not easily done either. Again, there is no one right answer. Rather, I am emphasizing that it is different for everyone. The idea is for you to consider all options and come to a realization where you know what is right for you.

Sometimes there is a false sense of comfort when you visit college campuses with members of your own family, because you are with people that are familiar to you. I can remember visiting campuses with my own family, the excitement of touring the facilities, learning about all the school had to offer, and my favorite part was going to a local restaurant together for lunch or dinner. I could also remember being dropped off at school as a freshman, and the feeling of seeing my parents leaving me there for the first time. I felt nervous, scared, and excited as the realities of being away quickly started to sink in for the first time.

Let's look at the benefits of going to a school that is within driving distance of your family:

- **Weekend visits**. These can be important, especially early in freshman year, for mental health reasons.
- **Laundry and home-cooked meals**. Some colleges have great food; others leave a grease stain on their plates. Either way, you might get a strong hankering for your dad's barbeque or your mom's shirt stain removal services.
- **Quick access for medical emergencies**. You can remain on your parents' health insurance until you're 26 years old. While the clinic at your college or university should be free, anything that requires a trip to a hospital won't be. Given

the costs of our health insurance companies in the U.S., it could be astronomically cheaper to drive home to visit a doctor (and stay in-network on your parents' plan) than to go out-of-network at a hospital near your school.

The drawbacks of going to a school that is within driving distance of your family:

- **Helicopter parents**. They know that they eventually will need to let their children grow up, but many may resist this urge. Unfortunately, a short drive to your college or university means that they will continue intruding. They might even assume that this is high school 2.0, and begin calling administrators or your professors. This happens less at schools that are located more distant from home.
- **No geographical advantage**. Many schools will give priority to applicants from distant or underrepresented portions of the country. If you're a local student, you'll look like the majority of their other applicants, and you lose that leg up.

I want to be clear that I am not advocating for any particular solution. You can stay home and commute, you can enroll in a school that is driving distance from home, or you can choose a school that is an airplane ride away. But you must consider thoroughly what each of these options means to you.

This decision could become more complex if you are looking to major in something that is specialized, as there may not be as many colleges that offer your program of intended study. In that case, you may need to just accept whatever distance it is, and remind yourself that staying flexible is a part of life.

Once you identify what criteria is important to you in a college, the more likely you will be able to narrow your search and find the right fit. Ultimately, these are the questions that you must reflect on and ponder, because only you know your own truth and comfort level, and what you are looking for in a college education.

Would I be more successful at a larger university that may offer more options while including lecture-hall style classes? Or would I prefer a smaller college that generally provides a more intimate feel and more professor interaction?

When we think of an academic environment, the size of the campus is one of the first things we see, especially if you are able to visit campus. Do not take for granted the importance of recognizing the type of academic environment you prefer. Ask yourself: do I want to be on a larger campus, or do I prefer a smaller school? Some students prefer attending schools with larger enrollments and bigger campuses, while others are looking for a more intimate setting, or something in the middle.

Class size is another item to consider. But this is not necessarily easy to determine simply by visiting campus, unless you are able to see multiple classes in session. Sometimes, a required class in freshman year can have 200 students, while a specialized lab course in senior year could have less than 15 students—and both at the same school! It is good practice to ask about class size, and how much that changes over four years of college. The only real guarantee is that a small liberal arts college, such as Amherst College (Episode 260) with an enrollment of 1900 students, will feature almost totally small classes.

Much is made about going to a school with a favorable student-to-faculty ratio, and it is certainly a characteristic worth considering. After all, getting to ask questions of full professors—not teaching assistants—is a hallmark of great education. The problem is gauging the truth of the ratio across an entire school, and the size of a school's campus does not necessarily correlate to its student-to-faculty ratio. For instance, at the same university, the music school may offer a 1-to-10 student-faculty ratio, while the business school offers a 1-to-35 ratio. The only way to ascertain is to ask questions of the admissions representatives, as I've noted already.

My own undergraduate college, Stony Brook University (Episode 34), was a larger school that offered lecture hall courses when taking their core curriculum. (A core curriculum is a set of classes that all students are required to take regardless of course of study.) In those classes, I was sitting with a couple hundred students. I was expected to take what the professor shared from the lecture and process the material on my own, within study groups, or in smaller follow-up classes with the graduate assistant. However, when I took courses specific to my major, I was in smaller classes that mirrored my high school, with only 20 to 30 students in each class. As someone who grew up in an urban environment, and being used to larger crowds, I welcomed the larger class sizes in my core curriculum, because it offered me an opportunity to get to meet many new people on campus. Other students, however, may prefer a smaller class setting in which the classes mirror the number of students typically found in a high school. This type of environment can feature more class discussions amongst peers.

My oldest daughter, who grew up in a suburb, initially was convinced she wanted to attend a large university. I think she felt like a change of environment would be good for her.

Then we visited a large university campus. We were lucky to be able to arrive while classes were in session, and a turning point in her decision occurred when we entered a lecture hall, with multiple auditorium-style classes in session. Some students were literally sitting outside on the lobby floor listening to the lecture, either because they arrived late, or perhaps they preferred listening by laying down. My daughter turned to me and asked, "Dad, what is this?" I explained that utilizing this style of class is an efficient way for colleges to provide instruction to large numbers of students in classes that they were all expected to take regardless of their intended major.

My daughter was attending a modestly sized high school in suburbia, and she recognized that this was not the right school for her, as it was simply too big. Reflecting on that trip, she decided that she wanted a small- to medium-sized college, with smaller classes, while also determining that she wanted to be within two hours driving distance from home. So, she selected Fairfield University (Episodes 20 and 235). The experience illustrates the reason that school visits can be such an important part of finding the right fit.

For me, the larger school setting, Penn State University (Episodes 9 and 252), which was further from home compared to where she ended up attending, would have been more than fine. In fact, I loved it! We are all different. Again, there are thousands of colleges in the United States alone, and although there is a school for everyone, not every school is for everyone. You have to know yourself and be honest when answering these questions, as this will guide you in making the correct decisions based on your own needs and preferences.

Do I want to be in an urban, suburban, or rural environment? Is the surrounding area off-campus important to me in terms of safety, internship opportunities, shopping, restaurants, recreational activities, or other things?

Selecting the right location that best suits your own interests is an important part of the college selection process, which will hopefully help you thrive during your time at school. Don't underestimate the importance of considering the benefits of each location, while weighing them against your own preferences, and choosing a school in an environment that is suitable to your individual needs. Doing so will help your chances of finding the right school, which is obviously an important goal in the overall selection process.

There are three categories of locations:

- **Urban**. These colleges and universities are both located within a major city and are socially involved in the health of that city as well. Many public transportation options typically serve this type of school, providing students with a variety of professional and recreational opportunities. U-Penn (Episode 166) is located in the University City district of Philadelphia.
- **Suburban**. These colleges and universities are located just outside a major city. They are often less directly involved in the health of their community, and the most common form

of transportation is the automobile, though buses are usually available, as well as school-sponsored shuttles. The same urban professional and recreational opportunities are available to them, but at greater distance and effort. Emory University (Episodes 68 and 211), located in the northeastern suburbs of Atlanta, is a good example.
- **Rural**. These colleges and universities are located in towns or small cities, far from major metropolises. Sometimes they are the centerpiece of the town itself, such as Cornell University (Episodes 14 and 240), with a total enrollment of 16,000 in Ithaca, New York (population: 32,000). Others, like Oberlin College (Episode 217) in Ohio, literally sit in the middle of fields. There is usually close connection with the local community, but there are also far fewer off-campus opportunities.

During the podcast episodes, college admissions representatives whose schools are located in urban environments, or in the vicinity of a big city, highlighted the many cultural and recreational options available, along with the many internship opportunities which may lead to jobs after graduation. They spoke of their large alumni associations and networking opportunities, which of course appeals to many prospective students, as cultivating career opportunities after college is an important consideration for most. On the other hand, higher expenses are associated with being in or near a big city, which is something to consider as cost of living might be higher compared to attending schools in other environments.

If you are considering an urban environment, it is also worth reflecting upon a few aspects of your personality.

- Do you enjoy trees and grass? In some urban environments, such as lower Manhattan, you won't see much greenery at all.
- Do you need alone time, far from other people? Urban life may not be for you, given the population density of cities.

- Do you need to feel absolutely one hundred percent secure when walking off-campus? While several major universities in big cities secure their school perimeters very well, they oftentimes grapple with the problem of off-campus crimes.
- Do you like the idea of having a well-defined campus, period? Some schools, such as Fordham University (Episode 239) in New York, have a distinct green campus as a collegiate oasis in a dense urban environment. Others, such as New York University (Episodes 28 & 262), are fully integrated with the urban environment. Step out of a dormitory at NYU, and you will find yourself swept up on the streets of Manhattan.

Asking yourself these questions, in advance, is really important.

On the other hand, representatives from schools in a rural environment speak of the many recreational opportunities their schools and surrounding areas may offer such as hiking, boating, skiing and so much more. They highlight the benefits of being close to nature and the tight knit communities they are located in, while forming their own alumni networks. However, there will be fewer internship opportunities in schools located in rural areas compared to those in an urban environment. The admissions representative from St. Louis University (Episode 185) spoke about how that school's Midwestern location paradoxically makes it easier to find internships, because there is less competition than there is among the young strivers in Los Angeles or New York. This lack of competitiveness, she explained, also filters into the culture of her school, which is far less competitive than similar schools on the coasts. This is something else to consider while researching colleges.

If you are considering a school in a rural environment, it is worth reflecting upon some different aspects of your personality.

- Are you a person who enjoys school spirit? Many rural schools sit distant from anything, and collegiate social life revolves largely around football games and other on-campus events sponsored by the student activities committee. For instance, Purdue University (Episodes 144 and 263) has 52,000 students and great school spirit. The town in which it sits, West Lafayette, Indiana, only has 44,000 people, many of whom work at the university. This is what is known as a "bubble" school, meaning that you will feel nearly encased by the university, and it will be difficult to find a reason to leave campus.

- Do you suffer from FOMO (Fear of Missing Out)? Friends who go to college in urban environments will be posting photos from concerts that you will not easily be able to attend.
- Do you dislike driving, or do you not own a car? Other than the occasional bus, there is no other transportation option in rural areas. You'll have to depend on new friends and classmates.

Asking yourself these additional questions, in advance, is really important.

Schools located in a suburban environment can offer a balance between rural and urban environments. Many college admissions representatives we spoke to from schools in suburban areas explained their school's location as being within driving distance of a major downtown area, while highlighting the cultural, recreational, and internship opportunities that their suburban zones also have to offer. It is true that a suburban area can offer students a multitude of recreational and job opportunities, while being on a tranquil campus, as the suburbs are less crowded than urban environments.

I know of a colleague who grew up in an urban environment and decided to attend a college in a rural setting. The town was quaint and pretty, in the middle of a gorgeous mountain range. However, the town had only one traffic light, and very few options on the weekends. For him, the culture shock was too great. He transferred after only one year.

Again, this decision is heavily dependent upon you, the individual. Whether you decide to attend a school in an urban, suburban or rural environment, there is no one correct answer. Opinions vary, based on life experience, personal temperament, and outside pressures. Consider the opposite of my urban colleague who fled the rural college: a person who grew up in a rural area, went to school in an urban environment, and quickly transferred somewhere quieter.

In total, be true to who you are, and do not underestimate the importance of reflecting on the locations of where you want to attend school while being in an environment that best suits your needs.

———

Does the climate where my school is located matter to me? Do I study better in hot weather or cold weather? Which one will make me happier?

Just as the location of your college can shape your experience, the climate and seasonal changes in that area are also important to consider. Preferences for climate vary widely: some students enjoy cold weather and mountainous regions for activities such as skiing, while others prefer warmer climates. Additionally, some people appreciate the distinct seasonal changes, while others opt for areas with a more consistent climate throughout the year. Understanding these preferences can help you choose a college environment that aligns with your lifestyle and interests.

Take into account extreme conditions, and whether or not it's the right climate for you. There are many areas that can get really hot and humid, while others get extremely cold. Some schools in the United States and Canada have underground tunnels and skywalks to minimize the amount of time one has to go outside to travel from class to class and back to the residence halls in the winter. Other schools are located in areas that are desert like and can experience extremely hot and humid conditions. Schools in these areas provide students with adequate cooling systems in their dorms and classrooms, along with hydration stations and multiple shaded areas throughout their campuses. Please remember all of this if you visit a school in the summer or winter, while neglecting to think about the weather conditions during the other seasons. Be mindful of the weather conditions throughout the year and select a school that fits your needs.

Interestingly, climate change is also having an effect upon higher education. Rising temperatures and extreme weather events are disrupting school calendars and causing students to miss out on more classroom education than before. When applying to universities, you should take these items into consideration.

―――

Have I selected my major and am applying to schools that offer a competitive program in my chosen coursework? Or am I undecided and want to attend a school that offers many options to students who are undecided?

If you have an intended major, or are considering a few options, make sure you are applying to schools that offer those areas of study. It is surprising to see how many students attend schools, only to find out later that they don't offer their intended course of study. Selecting a school that has a strong reputation for your intended major, is certainly good practice.

If you are undecided, you're not alone. It is common for students to enter university without a specific major in mind. In fact, there are a lot of benefits to being undecided. It provides you the chance to explore your interests, and develop a diverse set of skills, so that once you do commit, you won't waste any time or money taking classes for a major that you abandon. If your college or university has a strong core curriculum, much of your first (and possibly second) year will be most likely occupied by completing those general requirements anyways. For this reason, many schools don't ask students to declare a major until their third year—and often, a part of that can be spent studying abroad, which could delay the decision even further.

Colleges are aware of all of this, and they do not discriminate against applicants who are undecided. It is not a negative, in any way. On the other hand, it can definitely help to state, for example, that you're planning to become some kind of a science major, or a liberal arts major. Gloria Darko, assistant director of admissions at Carnegie Mellon University (Episode 208), commented that "students don't necessarily need to know exactly what they want to study, but they do have to have a general idea of the program or general area that they want to study. This is because we're not just looking to see if they are a fit for the whole university, we're looking to see if they are a good fit for the program they applied to. And, when we are reviewing applications, that is something that we take into consideration."

There is another situation that you may want to consider, especially if you have a talent for STEM. Some STEM students find themselves caught between pursuing, say, physics or electrical engineering. At most universities, those two majors are not found in the same school. Physics is found in the School of Arts & Sciences, while electrical engineering is found in the School of Engineering. An important thing to know about engineering is that it is regarded as probably the most difficult major on any college campus, which is why it usually takes five years to complete, instead of the usual four.

Here is the important part: *it is very difficult to transfer from another major into an engineering major*. The rules vary by institution, but many universities either forbid it or place strict requirements on anybody attempting to do it. Keep in mind that if you were to successfully transfer to an engineering major in your second year, that would also mean a total of six years in undergraduate programs. Transferring in during your third year, if possible (not likely), could mean up to seven years in undergraduate. For all these reasons, if a person is considering electrical engineering, I would urge that person to apply to the School of Engineering as a first-year student. If admitted, give it a shot, and if it doesn't work out, it is very easy to transfer to the School of Arts & Sciences and pursue a regular science degree. Many people in fact decide that the rigor of engineering is not for them, both as students and later in life as professionals. It is no mark of shame to do so.

When picking a university to apply to, please consider your future major. In fact, there is a good case to be made for ignoring the name of the university, and focusing instead on the reputation of the program that you want to study. For instance, students interested in musical theater should look at the national rankings for that major, where they will see the names of schools such as Carnegie Mellon University (Episodes 47 and 208), the University of Michigan (Episode 12), and Syracuse University (Episodes 4, 5, and 109).

What if I had an IEP or 504 Plan while in high school? Does the college I am applying to offer support and resources to help me continue to be successful?

A common question that I ask admissions representatives during the podcast episodes is what support services they offer for students who may have had an Individualized Education Plan (IEP) or a 504 Plan while in high school. Every college explained that they have resources to help students with differing needs continue to be successful while on their campuses, though the extent and nature of these services will vary. Most colleges have an office dedicated to providing support, often called the Office of Accessibility or something similar. If this is something that you need, it is important for you to search for schools that have the best resources while advocating for yourself early to find the best fit for your individual needs.

One example of an extensive support program is Iona College's Comprehensive Assistance Program (CAP). We spoke about this program and more in episode 13 of the podcast. The Iona College Comprehensive Assistance Program (CAP) offers a range of services to students with various disabilities, including learning disabilities, ADHD, autism, and traumatic brain injuries. To be considered for CAP, students must submit a separate application along with several specific documents, including psychoeducational or neuropsychological reports, behavioral assessments, and letters of recommendation. For more details about Iona's CAP, and to access their virtual information sessions, visit the Iona College website and search for their Comprehensive Assistance Program.

If programs like these are important to you as part of your college search, keep these additional tips in mind, which I used with my own family to help find the right college fit:

Research support services. Begin by exploring the support services available at each college you are considering. Visit their website to gather details on their Office of Accessibility or similar department. Get acquainted with the resources they provide, including academic tutoring, counseling services, and assistive technology. Additionally, many colleges conduct in-person and virtual information sessions that can help you assess whether the level of support meets your needs.

Reach out early. Contact the Office of Accessibility at each college you're considering to discuss your specific needs and learn about their accommodation application process. I found that reaching out by phone or email was easy and that the staff was consistently helpful. Engaging early with these offices will provide insight into how accommodations are managed and is crucial for ensuring that you will have the necessary support throughout your college experience.

Understand the process. Some colleges, like Iona College (Episode 13), have their own application or documentation procedures for accommodations. It's crucial to be aware of these details to avoid delays in receiving the support you need. Be proactive in asking specific questions about each school's process and requirements. Understanding the procedures for every college you're considering is key to ensuring you get the support necessary for your success. Be sure to check each college's website for the most up-to-date information on their accommodation processes.

Consult with your high school counselor. If you have a high school counselor, they can help make recommendations, gather necessary documentation, and provide insights based on other students' experiences. Establishing a relationship with your counselor early is crucial, as they can offer valuable support throughout high school and the college application process.

For those without a counselor, you can still get the support you need. Start by checking each college's website for the latest information on their Office of Accessibility or similar department. Engaging directly with these offices is the best way to get the most accurate and up-to-date information on their accommodations offerings. This approach will help you make informed decisions and ensure you receive the support necessary for a successful college experience.

Advocate for yourself and plan ahead. Once you're admitted, ensure all necessary arrangements are made before classes begin. Being proactive is key to starting your college experience smoothly. Since college can be quite different from high school, prepare for any adjustments you might need. Keep in regular contact with the Office of Accessibility or similar department to facilitate a successful transition and ongoing support throughout your college journey.

By taking these steps, you can help ensure that you have the support you need to succeed in college.

Is joining a sorority or fraternity important to me? If so, do the schools I am applying to offer this opportunity?

Whether you join a sorority or fraternity is your own personal preference, but there are certain things that you should consider.

Becoming a member carries some advantages. You have a guaranteed family of brothers or sisters whom you can rely upon. This can provide emotional support, camaraderie, and social connections. You create lifetime friendships. It can also elevate your feeling of connection and service to something greater than yourself, since many frats and sororities engage in philanthropy and community service in their communities. As the Greek system also values leadership, joining one of these organizations can be a great way to express your talent for organization and management, especially if you know you're going to be pursuing a career that requires these skills.

Although it provides good opportunities for networking, it can be very time consuming, particularly when you are pledging. Speak to pledges that have done this, and ask about the time and financial commitments. You might be surprised by what you hear. There are usually dues to be paid, along with other expenses to remain as an active member. Furthermore, your social life in college will become much more structured and inflexible, as you will be expected to live and socialize nearly exclusively with the other members of your house.

There are many mandatory meetings, events, and other obligations that cannot be missed.

Many students decide not to pursue Greek life and join less structured student organizations and clubs instead. That is your personal preference. Reflecting on the type of social life you are looking for can certainly help you with the transition to college and is something that should not be overlooked. A good suggestion that came up in many of the podcast episodes is to follow the social media pages of student organizations you intend to join. Many of those pages will give you good insight into what the student organizations do, while helping you determine if it is right for you.

Occasionally, there is a trend among colleges and universities to reconsider or ban Greek life due to concerns about certain activities within fraternities and sororities. These concerns often arise from incidents involving excessive drinking, risky behaviors, or hazing practices that can jeopardize student safety and well-being. While such incidents are regrettable and do warrant scrutiny, it's important to recognize that they represent specific issues rather than defining the entire Greek life system. Researching the Greek life culture at potential schools can help you identify organizations that align with positive values and responsible behavior, ensuring a more supportive and enjoyable college experience.

Some schools simply do not offer Greek life, meaning that they do not have any sororities and fraternities. They do of course offer other opportunities to join student groups related to other interests. Knowing what types of activities are offered at the school, can be an important fact to ask about while deciding which school is the right fit. Again, there are no right or wrong answers, but please consider all of the options. I have two daughters. One attended a school with no Greek life (Fairfield University, Episodes 20 and 235), while the other is a proud member of her sorority at Sacred Heart University (Episodes 10 and 169).

During the college search process, finding a school that offered Greek life was not a priority for either of my daughters. The daughter that attended Fairfield University engaged in other activities to immerse herself in all that her school had to offer, while forming meaningful lifelong friendships and loving her college experience. She never felt that she somehow missed out on anything without a sorority. On the other hand, my other daughter is a proud member of her sorority, which became a significant part of her college experience as it provided her with a strong sense of community, leadership opportunities, and meaningful connections.

Both daughters, despite their different paths, found activities and friendships that enriched their college experiences and met each of their individual needs. They selected schools and activities that were the right fit for themselves. This illustrates that whether or not Greek life is part of a college, there are so many ways to engage with and enjoy campus life. Consider all available options, and always choose what aligns best with your interests and goals.

Am I interested in studying abroad? If so, where?

Most universities have study-abroad programs these days, though there are sometimes criteria such as a minimum GPA that must be met first. It's very common to head to Europe for a semester, though options in the Middle East, Asia, Africa, Australia, and elsewhere have been growing in popularity. Junior year is the most common time for students to go abroad.

Keep in mind that most majors encourage study abroad, while others quietly make it less feasible to do so. Engineering majors, with their many demanding courses, sometimes find it difficult to schedule a full semester abroad. In those cases, it is sometimes possible to find summer internships abroad instead.

Traditional study abroad programs are affiliated with a foreign university; students live in dormitories with the other students, or in nearby housing. Some are highly structured, self-contained programs in which the study abroad students are kept separate from the population and carried on weekly field trips for research or learning. Still others can be unusual, such as a Semester At Sea, which is an international study abroad program on a ship. Some study-abroad programs are better characterized as work-abroad programs, as students end up interning at foreign companies for several months while doing little to no academic work.

Is cost a factor? If so, are private schools, which are generally more expensive, an option for me? Do I need to find a job while on campus, and does the school offer a work study program?

When the admissions representatives spoke of their top pieces of advice that they would provide students and their families going through the college process, many discussed the importance of having the financial conversation early with your family. The cost of college is expensive and a major consideration for so many families. Knowing your college financial fit will help you through the search process, while helping to avoid any disappointment later. Some admissions representatives spoke about how every year students are accepted, only to find out that they can't afford the cost of attendance, emphasizing the importance of researching the financial aspect of college early.

One thing that all students and their families can use to educate themselves about the cost of college is to use the Net Price Calculator. Every college and university in the United States is mandated to provide this calculator on their websites. It exists, according to the U.S. Department of Education, to "allow prospective students to enter information about themselves to find out what students like them paid to attend the institution in the previous year, after taking grants and scholarship aid into account." The search tool can be found at https://collegecost.ed.gov/net-price.

After answering the questions for the first time, come back to them after a few days and refine your answers as necessary. Answering these questions openly and honestly will give you a clearer picture of what you are looking for in a college education, which will help you throughout the process.

Working with your family is of the utmost importance so that there are no surprises. Review the questions and your answers with them early and often, so that everyone in the process can gain more clarity in terms of what type of school is right for you and the family, especially when it comes to finances. Your family knows you well, and are likely helping you pay for your education. So, it is important to have open and honest conversations about the many options in terms of cost, living arrangements, distance, and anything else that is important to you as a family. Since the conversation regarding colleges can become overwhelming for families, a good piece of advice that we heard in the podcast episodes was to designate a weekly night when you speak about the college process. This is so it doesn't consume your every conversation at home and becomes too overwhelming.

School counselors are another tremendous resource in the process. Seek their advice early. They are a wealth of knowledge in terms of different school options and what they offer both inside and outside of their classrooms. Reviewing questions such as those listed above, can only help you and your school counselor gain more clarity in terms of what you are seeking in a college education, while helping to narrow your search and create a more balanced list of schools to apply to. In addition, your school counselor will likely write your letter of recommendation with an overview of all you've done throughout high school. So it is important for them to know you intimately in terms of your academic achievements, involvement with student activities, and other initiatives you have participated in outside of school. Cultivating the relationship with your school counselor, if you have one, should not be underestimated throughout the process.

Students who have recently graduated from your high school, or who live in your area, can be another great source of information, particularly if they attend a school that you are interested in applying to. Many high schools offer opportunities to speak with alumni who currently attend various colleges throughout the country. If they do, take advantage of these opportunities as you will get a firsthand account of college life at that particular school. If you are fortunate enough to have such an opportunity, ask them what surprised them about their college and what would they do differently if going through the process again. Hopefully, their reflections will provide you with insights to help you reach your own decisions. Should your school not offer such a program, ask your school counselor if they can help you connect with former classmates who attend a school you're interested in, to discuss their college experience. Many times, these students live in your neighborhood, so it may be up to you to reach out and see if they would be willing to speak with you.

CHAPTER 5
THE COMPONENTS OF A COLLEGE APPLICATION

ALTHOUGH MOST HIGH school students have not had to put together a marketing package for themselves, they should approach the college application in that fashion.

After all, the college application is exactly that: a marketing package whose purpose is to provide the best representation of who you are as a potential student and community member. As an applicant, it is important to understand that how you performed academically in your classes and what you chose to do with your time outside of the classroom are both very important in the admissions process.

In fact, many admissions representatives have told me that they look at your application holistically to provide a comprehensive review of your entire application. They try to determine whether you will be able to handle their coursework if selected to be on their campus. They try to see what kind of community member you will be and how you might contribute to their overall mission and philosophy.

It will benefit students to have clarity in terms of the purpose of each part of the college application, and how these components are meant to build upon each other, without repeating the same information throughout. Admissions representatives review hundreds, sometimes thousands, of applications. Your task is to create a seamless application, one that repeats no information. This will help them do their jobs better, which can have a good outcome for you. Ian Schachner, an admissions officer from Cornell University's ILR Program (Episode 14) stated it best when he noted that the overall application is "not about a good use of space, but the best use of space."

In the college application process, students should showcase their academic and personal achievements while providing evidence that will hopefully convince admissions representatives to admit them. Understanding what admissions representatives are looking for from each part of your application is essential to ensure that you represent yourself comprehensively, while including academics, extracurricular activities, achievements, interests and anything else that would help a college understand what you bring as a potential student. If a student has early knowledge of how to thoughtfully work on developing items such as their transcript, activity sheet, essays and more, they will work towards displaying the best version of themselves during the college application process. These are items that when thought of early, you have some level of control and may provide you with a better grasp to help showcase everything you have to offer both in the classroom and beyond. Later, we will talk about institutional priorities, which as applicants, we do not have much control over. Institutional priorities are the reason why so many deserving students are not admitted even though their profile might be the same or better than many of the admitted students. This can lead to frustration throughout the process.

Let's first take a look at the different components of the application and talk about what the colleges are looking for when reviewing each. This should give you a better understanding of how they need to build upon each other.

CHAPTER 6
THE TRANSCRIPT

THE MOST IMPORTANT component of the academic portion of a college application is the high school transcript.

After all, a good indicator of how you will perform academically once you're in college, is to look at how you performed while in high school. Admissions representatives want to ensure that they admit students who will be able to handle the academic rigors associated with their schools, so the transcript becomes a key component in the application review process. In fact, in schools that are test optional or test blind, the transcript is weighed even more heavily in the overall application review. It helps admissions representatives determine whether you could handle the coursework on their campuses.

Items included on a high school transcript may vary between high schools. But all of them provide a mostly comprehensive record of the student's courses throughout high school. These include courses such as:

- Advanced Placement
- International Baccalaureate
- Dual enrollment (usually through a local community college)
- Honors

- Regular classes

Final grades are recorded for each course, including the type of grading scale, whether it is weighted or unweighted, and class rank when available.

It is important to familiarize yourself early with what your high school includes on your transcript so that you are aware of what the colleges will see once your applications are submitted. Understanding at the beginning of high school how the transcript relates to the college application process is important for students to recognize so that they may produce the best possible representation of their academic abilities throughout their four years of high school. Work with your high school counselor yearly to select the best courses to showcase your academic abilities, while building ramps and challenging yourself to the best of your ability, and view your transcript with your school counselor to ensure that all courses and proper grades are accounted for before submitting your applications to college.

Admissions representatives will look for trends on the transcript in terms of course selections, grades, rigor, ramps built over time and whether a student challenged themselves based on the courses available at their high school. If there are honors or Advanced Placement courses available at your school, it is definitely in your best interest to enroll in a few (or many) of them. There are limitations: for instance, not all high schools offer Advanced Placement courses. That's not a problem. On my podcast, admissions representatives consistently report that they review your transcript based on the context of what your high school has to offer. So consider this scenario, which has come up often as a question in the podcast episodes:

- Student A attends a school that offers 26 different Advanced Placement courses or other opportunities through their International Baccalaureate Program.
- Student B attends a school in a neighboring district that offers only a handful of Advanced Placement courses, and limits how many of those courses students can take.

Will Student B find himself at a disadvantage? Admissions representatives have told me repeatedly: definitely not. They are evaluating students based on what was available to them, and whether they took advantage of those opportunities.

What this means for you: If you're on the fence about enrolling in an AP class, by all means do it. If they're not available at the moment, don't sweat it.

Some students panic because their grades dipped at some point during high school. This is certainly not a major hurdle, and can even be flipped into a positive. See, many of the admissions representatives spoke about the importance of explaining why there may have been a dip in your grades. Perhaps there was a personal family issue that occurred such as a divorce or death in the family, which didn't allow you to put your best foot forward in sophomore year. Maybe you took on too many advanced courses and began drowning, academically.

Regardless, in your application, you should explain why there was a dip. If not, you are leaving it up to the admissions representative to speculate as to why. Most importantly, the transcript will show an upward grade trend afterwards. If you recovered nicely from the bad semester, it will look favorable when your application is reviewed. Everybody loves a comeback story, and admissions committees are no different. The Common Application offers an "Additional Information" section where you are encouraged to speak about such circumstances to give the admissions representatives a clearer picture of you as a potential student. If you've experienced a dip in your grades, you should use this section to explain!

College admissions representatives become very familiar with school profiles. Your school profile lists all academic opportunities that students have available to them at their high schools. These include:

- General information about the high school such as its name, address, phone number, mission statement, philosophy, recognitions, etc.
- An overview of the curriculum, graduation requirements and types of courses offered. For example, how many college level courses are available to students such as Advanced

Placement, International Baccalaureate and/or Dual Enrollment courses, along with availability of other types of courses in the academic or elective areas, including honors and non-honors courses.
- Grade distributions and the grading scale used at the high school, including whether it is alpha or numeric, and its overall grade distribution amongst students. Some schools share the typical percentage of students who score an A, B, C, etc., on their school profile. Grade distribution is very important in the overall review process because some high schools do not provide class rank despite the fact that some colleges and universities really like to see it. So, if a school gives an A+ to a high percentage of their students, it may cause the admissions representative to look closer at other evidence of academic success where class rank is not made available.
- An explanation of weighted/unweighted grading practices. For example, Advanced Placement or International Baccalaureate courses may be given bonus points when used to calculate a students overall grade point average, since these courses are considered advanced and at the college level.
- Data related to standardized tests, and other assessments such as Advanced Placement exams including their average or mean scores.
- A summary of the graduation requirements broken down by the number of credits required in each subject area.

School profiles vary from school to school, but they offer an admissions representative or anyone who reads it a good snapshot of the student body. Becoming familiar with your school profile, which is shared with colleges to assist them in the application review process, is good practice to help ensure that you are presenting yourself in the best light within the context of what you have available at your high school. This is a resource that is usually available through your high school's website. If not, ask your school counselor for a copy as it will give you insight into how a college admissions representative may review your application based on the context of what you had available at your high school.

Another important item to understand on your school profile is how each course is graded and how your overall Grade Point Average (GPA) is calculated. Many schools use alpha grades, while others use numeric. The scales these grades are calculated on vary as reported by the admissions representatives who shared that schools use scales on a 4, 8, 10, or 100 point scale, just to name a few. Equally important is knowing which courses are weighted in your high school: do they provide the weighted or unweighted GPA, or both? This is a good question to ask college admissions representatives when on campus or at a college fair. College admissions representatives from Carnegie-Mellon University and Emory University have reported to me that though they see an applicant's ninth grade courses, they don't use those grades in their overall recalculation of the student's GPA, though they do consider those grades as a part of their holistic review.

This was a typical question I asked throughout the podcast episodes, and it is a good one to ask when you are meeting with a representative for a college you are interested in attending, so that you get a clear idea of how they are looking at your GPA.

One overlooked resource is the humble high school counselor. This person is typically overworked, assigned a load of students far greater than anybody should ever have to assist. But that person can guide you in selecting classes that will lead to a college acceptance, which is especially valuable in highly competitive majors such as engineering, nursing, or musical theater. (Performance-based B.F.A. programs, which stand for Bachelor of Fine Arts, are tough to get into.) At the very least, that counselor can map out a path for you to take, academically, to make sure that you squeeze all the requirements, and then some extra classes, into your four years.

One other note: Many colleges require that you self-report your grades on your application. If you are applying with the Common Application, you can do this either on the Common App directly, or through a tool called SRAR (Self-Reported Academic Record). The SRAR is a detailed summary of all your academic work, and it eliminates the need for a transcript during the initial application phase. When you fill it out once, it can be used repeatedly with any schools that require it.

Some students question why they need to self-report grades at all. Doing so smooths out and quickens the process, since colleges can review applications more rapidly without the need for official transcripts. Later, in February and March, the school only needs to examine the transcripts of the students who have been admitted. This saves them a lot of time and effort.

Admissions officials who stick around for a few years will often get to know the school profiles of their regions quite well, and some long-term high school counselors have cultivated relationships with admissions offices at certain colleges or universities.

As mentioned earlier, the college admissions representatives commonly used the word *holistic* to describe how they review transcripts. This means that they are looking at all aspects of the transcript as opposed to just one, the same way a doctor would perform a holistic review of a patient as opposed to, say, liver function only. Therefore, when reviewing an applicant's transcript, admissions committees look at multiple items such as the GPA, courses selected over four years of high school, grades received for each course, credits earned, and class rank where applicable, just to name a few.

Let's look at an example of this in action. Consider the following two students who have applied to the same school:

- **Student A** has a 4.0 unweighted GPA, but he has taken no honors or advanced classes.
- **Student B** has a 3.6 unweighted GPA, but she has taken five honors and three AP classes.

If the admissions representatives looked at Student A's GPA in isolation, without considering course selection, he looks like the more attractive applicant. But this could be inaccurate as the GPA alone is not telling the entire story related to his overall academic achievements. He never selected any of the rigorous courses that the high school offered. He chose to prioritize other aspects of his education, for whatever reason.

Meanwhile, if the admissions representatives looked at Student B's GPA in isolation, without considering course selection, she looks like the less attractive applicant. But this is almost certainly inaccurate as, once again, the GPA alone isn't telling the entire story. Student B selected no less than eight rigorous courses. That says a lot about her ambition, her willingness to challenge herself, and the likelihood of her future success.

Admissions officials carefully review applications for these types of differences between applicants.

A word about weighted GPAs: High schools often provide bonus points to students' GPAs for having taken courses such as Advanced Placement or International Baccalaureate. A weighted GPA is a high school's way of calculating and accounting for all the bonus points, usually for college-level or rigorous courses. The specific courses that receive bonus points, and what is weighted, vary by high school. This is why many of the college representatives I've spoken to report that their universities often recalculate GPAs in a good-faith attempt to level the playing field.

After all, there is no consistent system throughout all high schools, nationally, in terms of which courses are offered or how they are weighted. Some use a 4-point scale, while others use a 10-point or 100-point scale. Some use alphabetical grades, while others use a numerical grading system. In all cases, the character of the high school itself is considered strongly in the decision. "We review the academic curriculum through the lens of the student's high school," said Barkley Barton, associate dean for evaluation and selection at the University of Pennsylvania (Episode 166). "I think I need to say that again. We review the academic curriculum *through the lens of a student's high school.*"

Furthermore, many of the admissions representatives indicated in our podcast conversations that grades in core academic subjects like math, science, social studies, and English are sometimes given more weight by admissions representatives than grades in elective classes. Therefore, an excellent question to ask a college admissions representative is whether they look at your high school's weighted or unweighted GPA, and whether they re-calculate the GPA using their own metrics.

This does not mean that you must only take the most difficult courses during your time in high school, but it is important to show growth and how you matured. I call this building ramps. For example, taking English Honors in 9th and 10th grades may lead you to build enough confidence to sign up for AP Language in 11th grade. Those first two courses serve as a ramp to a higher level of learning.

Keep in mind also that some schools, such as the entire University of California system, do not consider your ninth-grade classes as part of your GPA. Leticia Garay, assistant director of admissions at UC-Davis (Episode 71), said, "We are using a GPA, but it is not as shown on your transcript. This applies to the entire UC system. We calculate our own GPA using grades earned from summer after ninth grade all the way through summer after eleventh grade. We still ask for students to report ninth and twelfth grade courses and grades for ninth grade, but we use them more as a trend, to see how the student has progressed through their years."

If you want to stand out from the pack, one thing you could do is take more than the required number of years for a particular subject, especially if it's in the major that you think you might choose in college. For example, in New York State, students are required to take a minimum of three years of mathematics and science. Taking a fourth year would send a message, particularly for STEM applicants, that they have gone beyond the minimum, and are serious about their education.

Based on your intended major and/or the type of school you are applying to, admissions representatives may look to see how you performed in specific types of courses. For example, if you are interested in the STEM fields (science, technology, engineering, and math), admissions representatives have reported to me the importance of having completed physics, chemistry, pre-calculus/calculus, and others. In fact, if a student has a particular major in mind, a good question to ask an admissions representative is which courses should be completed in high school, or be in progress during senior year, to help increase their chances of being accepted. The earlier you ask this question, the sooner you will understand these nuances which will help you create a stronger application if you intend on applying to a specific major that is more competitive.

In the end, though, all courses are somewhat important in the eyes of admissions committees, even for subjects that hold little interest to the applicant. Admissions representatives, and college administrators in general, want to make sure that nursing majors can communicate adequately, that history majors can do some math, and that biology majors have some media literacy.

At the very least, if you are college bound, my suggestion would be to consider taking at a minimum one college-level course by the time you are in junior or senior year. This will again vary by student, but showing that you tried one advanced course by the time you graduate high school should help your overall application, depending of course on the selectivity of the college you are applying to.

Furthermore, remember to keep putting your best foot forward through your last year of high school. I like to remind students to not underestimate the importance of senior year courses. Depending upon the deadlines, your first-semester senior-year grades may or may not be available at the time you are submitting your applications. Eventually, however, the admissions representatives will see your grades in those courses, and you never know if those grades will come into play later, should you get deferred or waitlisted.

In fact, one of the more unsavory facts about college admissions is that many colleges and universities may withdraw acceptance offers from students who experience second-semester senior year GPA drops. For decades, the University of California system annually withdrew approximately 2% of its acceptances for this reason. That must be a terrible feeling, like tripping over your own track shoes just short of the finish line.

The lesson here is clear: senioritis can have serious consequences. Stay focused and maintain your effort until the end!

If you find yourself struggling academically, keep in mind that you are not alone. Achieving great things takes a lot of work and time to do so. Be mindful of seeking help early and often, as there are many resources available to you. You have excellent resources to seek help from: teachers, school counselors, tutors, and even other students serving as peer tutors. In fact, forming peer study groups in challenging courses is a great and affordable way to work through whatever academic issues you may face. Showing this type of initiative is also a great way to demonstrate leadership abilities, since you'll be helping not only yourself but also others.

My final observation: Although many schools report reviewing applications in a "holistic" manner, a student's transcript is still the most important piece of the application, as indicated by many of the admissions representatives. Consider it as the first among equals.

CHAPTER 7
EXTRACURRICULAR ACTIVITIES

AS PART of their holistic review process, college admissions representatives are very interested in knowing what you do with your free time after school. The extracurricular activities you participate in will provide college admissions representatives with a good indication of your interests. Just like your past academic performance is an indicator of how you may perform in college classes, the after school activities you participate in will help demonstrate the type of classmate, roommate, and contributor you will be to their school community, which is an important factor for admissions representatives who are trying to put together an incoming freshman class.

As a student, you should try to participate in activities that are in line with your interests, making a stronger case for your particular profile that you're presenting to college admissions committees. Admissions representatives not only want to know which activities you participated in, but what was your motivation for doing so. Although the Common Application limits the number of characters you may use in the descriptions on the Activities section, be mindful about explaining your motivations in as much detail as possible.

In speaking with the college admissions representatives on my podcast, I heard a consistent message: nobody is looking for a particular activity. Rather, colleges want to see that you made good use of your time and have explained what you did with it.

This doesn't only include teams and competitions. Extracurricular activities also include having a part-time job or taking care of a family member. In many episodes of my podcast, it was emphasized how important it is to include jobs and other family responsibilities, which limits other types of traditional college-bound extracurriculars. Andrea Flores, assistant director of recruitment at Florida State University (Episode 213), said, "For some students, extracurricular activities can be those traditional things like clubs, sports, things like that. But for other students, we know that circumstances are different. And so this could also involve employment. It could be family responsibilities that a student has, community service that they're a part of—whatever they're doing outside of the classroom is really what we want to see here. A big thing for us at FSU is that we never want to penalize a student for something that is outside of their control."

Such activities give an admissions review team a lot of insight into who you are as a person, since holding a job requires you to report to work on time and answer to a supervisor, and since caring for a family member requires empathy and loyalty. For instance, due to language barriers, some students have to accompany parents or family members to medical appointments, and these are all important skills for the admissions representatives to know about. After all, not everyone is able to demonstrate this level of responsibility and commitment while in high school. So, if this pertains to you, remember to explain it in your application, rather than leaving it up to an admissions representative to speculate as to why you are not involved with academic, athletic, or volunteer extracurricular activities.

The admissions representatives recommended approaching the extracurricular activities with an attitude of quality over quantity. In other words, it is better to be part of a few extracurricular activities throughout high school, where you can show your growth and leadership skills, rather than having a long list of activities with little substance in terms of your involvement. Sometimes students first realize that listing extracurricular activities is part of the college process as late as 11th grade, and so they begin participating in a flurry of activities right near the end of high school, just to fill their list. College admissions representatives see right through this, so I can't emphasize enough the importance of being aware of this before the start of high school, so that you can ultimately present yourself in the best light when it's time to apply to college.

Many high schools will emphasize the importance of getting involved in activities outside of the classroom. High schools may even make doing so a graduation requirement or a criterion to be inducted into the National Honor Society. This helps ensure that the students are growing and becoming more well-rounded outside of the classroom, while also helping them with the activity sheet portion of their college application.

Be sure to list the progression of any leadership roles throughout your four years of high school, as this can add to your overall application. This does not mean that you have to be the president of a club, as not all students can serve in this position. Rather, be mindful that leadership comes in many forms. Perhaps you spearheaded a clothing drive for one of the clubs you are directly involved in, or maybe you created a tutoring program as part of your athletic team for younger players. Be creative! There are many things that you can do to demonstrate leadership, and don't underestimate the importance of doing the things you like.

A nursing student from Episode 145 also shared how while in high school, she volunteered at a clinic and nursing home, which likely helped her overall application. At the same time, she learned as part of her on-the-job training that she in fact wanted to pursue the field of nursing. Realizing that you want to pursue a particular major based on your field work, and then articulating this experience, can only help you. Remember that admissions representatives want to admit students that will matriculate and stay in their programs, so demonstrating real world experience in a field you intend to pursue is a net positive.

Having a nursing internship while in high school can help you in the college process. Admissions teams may look favorably upon the fact that you were exposed to the work of a nurse, and are still pursuing it as a major and career. This can be a benefit in the competitive application review process, since colleges and universities want to admit students who have demonstrated that they can do the work, but also who are likely to graduate. That data is important to the colleges.

Another way to think about extracurricular activities is to break them down into two pairs of groups. One pair is individual vs group extracurriculars. Look at your list of activities, divide them into solo vs. team activities, and see if you naturally gravitate to one type or the other. If so, perhaps think about trying something from the other side. For instance, if all your activities are solo tennis, solo studying, and solo volunteering, look for a team-based activity. The opposite is also true: if all your activities are group-oriented, try to expand into something that permits you some alone time. Taking online courses at edX or Coursera is an easy way to do this. (Be sure to get the certificate at the end of the course, if offered, so you can present it to colleges as proof if needed.)

The other pair of groups is pre-existing vs. self-started. In other words, many extracurricular activities existed before you entered high school, and they will continue to exist after you leave high school. This includes most clubs, sports teams, and other things. On the other hand, a self-started extracurricular activity is something that didn't exist before the student decided to invent it. This can include creating brand-new clubs, tournaments, or initiatives. This can include writing and self-publishing your first book, or starting your own podcast. Most high school students participate in pre-existing activities, which is perfectly fine, but if you're aiming at a high-level ultra-selective school, building a new activity out of nothing, or starting a brand-new initiative out of an existing club, is one way to do it. This is the more difficult path, however. Founders often encounter many obstacles, from school administration to lack of funds to logistics problems to difficulty recruiting members. Don't let that discourage you. If you want to do something, do it! It can also serve as an excellent topic for a personal statement: your idea, the obstacles you encountered, your reflections, and the questions you pondered. Explain how you adapted to challenges, how the experience shaped who you are today, and what you plan to do with the lessons you learned.

We spoke about building ramps in your academic journey in terms of the courses you selected throughout high school, as admissions representatives look for upward trends in your academic life and your extracurricular life. This is a good indicator that you will be able to do the work once you are sitting in their classrooms. Equally important is your commitment to a few diverse activities, while demonstrating to admissions representatives how your involvement in them has evolved throughout high school.

Take initiative. Show your leadership abilities throughout your activities. If you don't want to be the founder of a new club, then start a new initiative within an existing club and bring people together to bring your idea to fruition. Show your organizational abilities and creativity. Nobody has all the desirable characteristics in the world, but we all have at least one. Figure out which are yours, and highlight them.

Still, always remember to find the right balance between the time you need to keep up with your academics, while displaying consistent and meaningful participation in the activities you enjoy.

CHAPTER 8
STANDARDIZED TESTS

STANDARDIZED TESTS such as the SAT and ACT represent another academic portion of the college application.

Where the transcript shows course selections and various trends throughout high school, a standardized test score represents a single performance on a single day. It's a data point, not a graph. Still, that doesn't stop many students from panicking and preparing—or over-preparing—for their shot at a perfect score.

How significant are these exams in the college admissions process? The truth is that their importance can vary. While students may place a great deal of emphasis on them, admissions committees might weigh them differently, often considering them as just one of many factors in the decision-making process as we have learned in the podcast episodes.

During the covid-19 pandemic, many colleges and universities recognized that students were unable to take a standardized test. Many testing centers closed for months, and it would have been unfair to punish those who couldn't access them, or didn't want to for health reasons. As a result, most colleges and universities instituted a test-optional policy.

The immediate result was a huge spike in applications to Harvard, Yale, Princeton, etc. Thousands of students were encouraged to pursue admission to the most exclusive universities in the world.

Another effect was the creation of a test-blind policy at the University of California. This was life-changing, since the UC system had been the biggest recipient of standardized tests in the entire country.

So, what do all these changes mean for you?

It's true that many schools have gone test optional. However, my expert opinion is that students should still prepare for these exams. They can help you, especially if you achieve a score that is within the school's middle 50% (defined as the range of scores that fall between the 25th percentile and 75th percentile) or even higher. That data is easy to find for any college or university, because the middle 50% happens to be the range of scores that colleges and universities publicly release anyways.

Let's be clear: if you fall within the mid 50% range or higher, and feel that your scores accurately portray who you are as a student, it is advisable to submit your scores to that school. Achieving this goal, would provide an admissions team with another piece of evidence that you are prepared to take on the challenges of a college education. If you fall lower than the mid 50% range, admissions representatives generally advise not to submit those scores. This is especially true if your transcript tells a better story than your standardized tests. On the other hand, if you are happy with your scores, particularly if they are consistent with your course grades or help improve your overall evidence of academic performance, then submit them.

There is another reason why you may want to submit standardized test scores to a test-optional university. Some colleges and universities are finding out that students who submit standardized test scores perform better in their first year than students who did not. Exhibit A: The University of Texas at Austin (Episode 63). In March 2024, the admissions committee announced its decision to reinstate mandatory standardized tests for all undergraduate applicants. The reason: their internal analysis found that the freshmen who had submitted test scores earned a GPA that was 0.83 points higher than those who did not. In other words, they were better academic students. The university noticed and began limiting admissions to those types of applicants. While this story may not repeat exactly at every school in the country, the pattern will nonetheless be present elsewhere.

However, if you choose not to submit your scores to a school that is test optional, the admissions representatives indicated that they would review all other parts of your application as part of their holistic review. They would place more emphasis on items such as your transcript, which represents the greatest indicator of your academic performance on your application. It's also important to keep in mind that the middle 50 percent scores are now higher in schools that are test optional, because only students that score well on standardized tests are submitting. The entire range has skewed upwards as a result of test-optional policies.

There are many reasons why standardized tests benefit you in the overall admissions process. Strong scores can certainly help an admissions representative determine whether you have the academic abilities to perform well in their school's environment. Don't forget that standardized tests have been used to predict future academic success for decades, especially the reading sections. On the other hand, if you are not a strong test taker—and you aren't alone, believe me—schools that are test optional will use other factors to determine whether you get accepted. These include your transcript, extracurricular activities, letters of recommendation, and personal statement.

Remember that if a school is test optional, it may still require scores for some of their more competitive majors, such as engineering or nursing. Be sure to do your own research when applying to schools by searching their websites, or speaking to an admissions representative directly. Another important question to ask admissions representatives at test-optional schools is whether or not their schools use standardized test scores to award scholarships. On my podcast, many of the admissions officials commented that they use other factors, such as the transcript, to help award academic scholarships when test scores are not submitted. However, this isn't always the case, so it's always best practice to ask.

One other option for standardized testing is something called "test-flexible". What does this mean? Test-flexible schools such as Lehigh (Episode 207) and Emory University (Episodes 68 and 211) will consider other tests if you wish to submit them, such as AP exams or IB scores. This is a nice compromise, and it's nothing unusual. Cambridge University in England holds a similar policy: it will accept applicants from a British curriculum, from an International Baccalaureate curriculum, or from an American curriculum as long as a high standardized test score is submitted, along with at least five AP exams, all of which must exhibit a perfect score of 5. Flexible but challenging!

Many students and parents believe that schools claiming to be test optional are being disingenuous. I disagree. Throughout recording hundreds of podcast episodes, I have learned that in most cases, the percentage of acceptances is fairly evenly divided between those who don't submit test scores and those who do.

- The admissions representative from Vanderbilt University (Episode 26), a very competitive school, reported that 45 percent of the previous year's class applied without submitting test scores, and the same percentage of students were admitted without scores.
- The admissions representative from Carnegie-Mellon University (Episode 208), another very competitive school, reported that the percentage of students who applied and were admitted without submitting test scores was between 35 percent and 40 percent.
- The admissions representative from Syracuse University (Episode 50) reported that 60 percent of the previous year's class submitted applications without test scores, and closer to 70 percent of those students were admitted.
- The admissions representative from Michigan State University (Episodes 7 and 50) reported that 55 percent of

the students applied without submitting scores, and the same percentage was admitted.

Do you remember my advice about submitting your test score if you fall within the middle 50 percent of the school's publicly released range or higher? That wasn't pulled out of nowhere. Many of the people I interviewed on my podcast reported the same thing: if your test scores fall within the middle 50 percent range or higher, and you feel that they would add positively to the overall academic portion of your application, submit them. If not, don't feel an obligation, but of course make sure your transcript is strong in terms of rigor and upward progression over the years. This is especially true if you are applying to some of the most competitive schools. Ask yourself whether your transcript tells a better story without the test scores. If so, don't submit the scores.

Another interesting development: The middle 50 percent ranges that schools are reporting are skewed compared to their numbers prior to the covid-19 pandemic. For the most part, it seems that only those students who are comfortable with their scores are submitting, which creates a higher middle 50 percent range compared with prior. Don't forget that 25 percent of admitted students fall higher than the reported mid 50 percent, while another 25 percent score lower. It's very possible that they were strong in other parts of their application, such as the rigor of coursework completed in high school, along with their overall grades as seen on their transcript.

If you are applying to a specific major or school within a university, it is important to ensure that tests are optional for the specific program, where tests are optional for the general population applying to that school. We discussed in many episodes that although a school might be test optional for its general application pool, it is important to see if their more competitive programs, such as nursing or engineering, require that tests be submitted.

———

It's worth touching on the concept of yield.

With the increase of schools going test optional, colleges and universities are receiving more applications than ever before, though their number of available seats is not rising at the same proportion. With the additional applications, it's becoming ever so difficult to determine what percentage of accepted applicants intend to matriculate (yield). As discussed in the podcast episodes, this process involves a high degree of uncertainty and estimation. Universities have always attempted to peer into their crystal balls to estimate just how many of their acceptances will turn them down and attend college elsewhere. Making this estimate is one of the most important tasks a college or university has to do.

In short, schools feel pressure not to accept more students than they can comfortably house, feed, and educate. As a result, schools grow cautious, sending out fewer acceptances than before, and putting more students on waitlists. A university's worst nightmare is ending up with more student enrollments than there are seats available, which happened to the University of California-Irvine in 2017. The university was forced to rescind admissions to 500 excited freshmen, which was a public relations nightmare.

Each year colleges have a projected yield, or a percentage of accepted students that they think will matriculate. For example, if a school needs 1000 students to fill their class, and their yield is 40 percent, it has to accept 2500 students to yield that 1000 student class. There are institutional research groups that help keep track of the yield data each year. There are also institutional goals they must fulfill, which vary by program, such as seeking more students who apply to a particular major, or are from a certain geographic area. Schools sometimes use the waitlist as a means to fill these institutional needs as part of their overall process.

It's worth recognizing that applicants aren't always in the driver's seat, and that a rejection is rarely personal.

The counterpart to the yield is something known as retention. This refers to the percentage of students who return to that college in the second year. Nationally, that percentage is perhaps lower than you think: only 68.2 percent for students who began college in 2022. Much of that is due to low retention rates at community colleges, which average only 55 percent from first to second year. At four-year colleges and universities, the average retention rate is typically around 80 percent.

You can understand how important this number is to admissions representatives. Every student who leaves their school is another lost customer, and that means lost revenue, so they want to retain as many students as possible. This number should also be important to you, because a school's retention rate reflects its attractiveness. A high retention rate generally promises better student outcomes, so it is worth your time and attention to find this number when making your college list.

So, which standardized exam should you take: the SAT or the ACT?

The digital SAT has two sections: Math, and Reading and Writing. Each one has two modules. It's an adaptive-by-module exam, which means that how you perform on the first math module determines the difficulty of the second one. The same goes for the reading and writing modules.

The ACT, meanwhile, is also digital, but it has four different sections: English (which is mostly grammar), Math, Reading, and Science (which is mostly data). It's not adaptive by section; the exam is fixed.

The primary differences are that the SAT is shorter and slower than the ACT. It features 154 questions, while the ACT features 215 questions. The SAT also tests fewer topics than the ACT. There is no science section on the SAT, and its range of grammar errors tested is narrower than on the ACT. Finally, the SAT reading has no long passages, which tend to be difficult for students to understand, while the ACT has four long reading passages.

Based on that description, you may be thinking that the SAT is the obvious choice, but let me caution you that it's not quite that easy. Because the SAT is so short and streamlined, every question counts for more towards your score. There is less leeway, which means more pressure. Taking the ACT is a bit looser: you can afford to miss more questions, but at the same time you do need to work faster.

If you are talented at scanning tables and graphs about scientific things, then you might want to take the ACT. If you enjoy reading through long texts looking for evidence, then consider the SAT. Lastly, if you're always one of the first people in your class to finish an exam, then you should think about taking the ACT. Still, I suggest that students take practice tests for both exams in order to see which one they are more comfortable with.

Don't worry about which exam colleges or universities prefer. None of them have any specific test preference. Also, feel free to take the exam once or twice, perhaps even three times. More than that isn't recommended: studies have consistently shown that student scores hit the ceiling after the third attempt.

Students also often overestimate the amount of impact that an SAT or ACT score can have. It's nowhere near as important as the transcript or the degree to which you've challenged yourself. Tim Fields, senior associate dean of undergraduate admissions at Emory University (Episode 211), told me: "Too many times applicants get bogged down on testing. I can assure you that in my 20 years of doing this, testing was never a determiner of whether a student was admitted."

If that is true at Emory, it is certainly true elsewhere as well. Keep everything in perspective.

CHAPTER 9
THE PERSONAL STATEMENT

ASIDE FROM TAKING (or retaking) standardized exams and enrolling in courses for your senior year, the only other part of the application over which rising seniors have direct control is the personal statement.

In this, it's important to remember not to merely repeat something that is easily found in other parts of your application, such as your transcript or your list of activities. This would be a missed opportunity. Your personal statement needs to build upon your "marketing package", providing something new about you to the college admissions committee. In fact, if an admissions representative finishes your essay without learning anything new about you, it would be a big miss on your part. So, when your personal statement is in draft form, ask others to read it. Ask if they learned anything new about you. If they have not, you need to rethink either the topic or the expression of your ideas.

The personal statement is an opportunity for you to use your authentic voice to share a story, while giving insight to the college admissions representatives into your motivations, your personality, and other reflections. I want to emphasize here that the personal statement is about using your genuine voice and being true to who "you" are, as many admissions representatives reported that they can tell when a personal statement was written by a student applying to college, as opposed to someone else writing it for you. We have heard the warnings multiple times that you do not need to use words that you wouldn't use in everyday language.

One technique that many find helpful is to read your personal statement out loud while recording it on your phone. Then, during the playback, you can listen to the strengths and weaknesses of the writing. This can also help you find your authentic personal voice.

The arrival of artificial intelligence tools has created a new problem: applicants using AI to write their personal statements for them. That is one of the silliest ideas I've ever heard. There is no way on earth that any AI tool will be able to write about your life better than you can. You alone have the personal experience and knowledge needed to portray your life to the admissions officials. AI can't capture the specific details that make your story unique to you, so stay away from it.

There are other reasons to avoid AI. The biggest one is that colleges have already prohibited the use of such tools, and their applications are run through AI-detection tools. While these tools are somewhat unreliable, they may become more reliable in the future. Despite the prohibition, students who decide to still use these tools to somehow "improve" their application are risking denial of acceptance. In short: avoid AI like the plague as a substitute for original writing.

The essay should tell a story that will help them gain a better understanding of who you are as a person, and why they would want you on their campus, in their dormitories, and in their classrooms. If your essay is about a specific event, or someone who influenced you, it is essential that you include how this affected you as a person. What was your reflection process about whatever it is that you are describing? What were the questions you asked yourself? What were some of your struggles, and how did you overcome them?

It was reported throughout the podcast episodes that too many applicants explain a story, or a person in their lives that influenced them, while neglecting to speak about these more important things. So please avoid this common mistake. Understand that admissions representatives read dozens of essays each day when they are reviewing applications. If you want to stand out, avoid writing about the typical themes talked about in the podcast episodes, unless you're able to take a unique spin on things while expressing your thought process, reflection, how you pivoted, and ultimately how it helped shape who you are today.

Pick a topic that is important to you and tell a story, in your way of using language, that will demonstrate something new about your life.

You may be asking yourself: How can I go about selecting a topic for the personal statement?

It's a fair question. Choosing a topic for the personal statement is one of the most difficult things for some students to do.

Let's start by defining what *not* to do.

In the podcast episodes, I learned that the most common topics selected by applicants included sports injuries and family members. Mission trips to help disadvantaged people are another perennial favorite. It's true that, if written well, any of these topics can deliver a very personal and well-done statement. However, that is more likely with a topic that the admissions officials haven't read a few hundred times. Remember that they are people too, and your first job is not to bore them.

For instance, too often students write about how much they love a sport, how they got an injury, and how they couldn't play anymore. If that's all your personal statement says, it's not enough. That sends a very basic message: *I had something, I lost it, now I'm sad*. This is too simple, and it can be true of everyone on earth. Instead, dive deeper into self-reflection, the questions to be pondered, and ultimately how you grew from the related challenges and experience. How did getting injured change you? What did you really lose, and what did you really gain? What were your complex emotions surrounding the injury? Exploring these deep emotions and reflections in your personal statement can lead to profound insights and a more compelling narrative.

Another common cliche is the so-called grandmother essay. It's quite common for a student to write a beautiful elegy for a deceased grandparent, or a gorgeous appreciation for a living one. Neither works very well as a personal statement. The simple reason is that the writing usually ends up being all about the grandparent, not the applicant, who remains invisible. As Jua Howard, assistant director of admissions at University of California-Berkeley (Episode 206), said, "If you want to talk about a loved one, I love those responses. But it needs to be 10 percent about that person, 90 percent about you. Set up who the person is, the dynamic of your relationship, and then you need to shift it back to your point."

There are a few times when this suggestion can be ignored, perhaps when a grandparent has had an enormous effect upon the applicant's life, but those tend to be the exception to the rule. If the topic must be about a grandparent, the personal statement needs to address how the applicant was inspired by and grew from their relationship. Speak less about the grandparent and focus the essay on how it affected you and your own reflections.

The mission or relief trip is another common topic for the personal statement. For many high school students, a trip to Central America to work with disadvantaged people in a village for a week or two is an eye-opening experience. For those students from somewhat wealthy families, this may be their first realization that poverty is real, and it's difficult for those afflicted by it. Those are great lessons to learn, but in that case, what will be the message of the personal statement? *I went to Guatemala, I met poor people, wow I am so lucky.* You have to be really careful not to come off as spoiled, or out of touch with how the world really works. Simple gratitude for home and family is okay, but that theme has been delivered thousands of times. If you decide to do a topic like this, please remember that the message you deliver needs to be more sophisticated, to counteract the simplicity of the topic.

Another area to be cautious about: friendship groups changing, especially in the transition from middle school to high school. It's quite normal for friendship groups to be fluid for many people in high school, and talking about navigating those changes probably won't make you stand out. As usual, there are exceptions to this trend, especially for people with an exceptional amount of emotional intelligence and insight into personal relationships.

Furthermore, in the heart of the application review season, admissions representatives may read dozens of essays per day, so it would be beneficial to write about something that is not so common. A simple topic with a unique message may help your overall application during their review process. Gloria Darko, assistant director of admissions at Carnegie Mellon University (Episode 208), said, "The essays that have stuck the most with me weren't necessarily because of the particular topics that students chose, but more because of the different values that I was able to learn that the students have."

So, what *should* you write about?

Let's move on to what you can select. Here are a few ideas to get the little hamster in your mind turning:

- **A big <u>external</u> challenge in your life.** These are often family problems: an illness, a job loss, a cross-country move.
- **A big <u>internal</u> challenge in your life.** This includes all the inner-directed emotional problems of daily life: coping with anxiety, dealing with heartache, struggling with a learning disability, etc.
- **A person you admire.** It could be someone you know, or someone you look up to from afar. A personal statement about a role model is a great way to show college admission officials what really matters to you. Still, make sure the vast majority of your personal statement is about you, not all about the person you admire.
- **Describe something you love**. If you're so passionate about potato chips that you could write 650 words of praise and analysis about Pringles, then by all means do it. In the end, the expression matters more than the topic. Comparing the aspects of your personality to the different ingredients in your family's beloved chicken pot pie recipe, for instance, would be a great way to go.

- **A time when you made a big mistake.** This might feel counterintuitive to those of you who think that you need to present a perfect version of yourself. But being honest about a time when you did something wrong helps to expose your inner workings.

In the end, don't give the admissions committee what you think they want to see. Don't present them with the glossy brochure version of yourself. Those things are fake. It's much better to be honest about who you are.

Michael Cameron, the Director of Admissions at the Rhode Island School of Design (Episode 110), gave an example of one of his favorite personal statements. An applicant wrote about Krispy Kreme donuts, how she loved going to a local shop to watch them being made. The twist in the story was that the applicant spoke of a donut that came out not quite the same as all the other donuts, so it was placed aside. The student proclaimed her desire for that donut: even though it looked different, it still tasted as good and brought the same amount of joy as did the other donuts. The analogy was made clear, and as a result it remained one of the most memorable personal statements that the director had read, to the point where he was sharing it publicly, in this episode of my podcast.

Try to think of experiences you've had thus far and make a list until something that feels right comes to mind. On the podcast, admissions representatives shared many more examples. A parent who drove the applicant to school each day, and the nature of the conversations evolving over time, showing the student's growth and maturity. Or a student's experience cooking with a parent and relating the different ingredients of what they were making to who they were as a person.

While the personal statement is important, what's more vital is how you use the topic to give deeper insight into who you are as an applicant. In other words, the topic is less important than how you deliver the personal statement itself. For this reason, when preparing to write your personal statement, consider the different elements of your personality, and your character, that you want the college to see about you. Then make sure those things are incorporated into your statement.

Ian Schachner from Cornell University (Episodes 14 and 127) spoke about the overall applicant pool. As an Ivy League university, of course, Cornell gets many personal statements from students listing amazing achievements. He explained that the applicants who stand out are those who don't just list their achievements, but who explain their journeys, and who make it clear that they have a lot more learning to do and more to accomplish. The mistakes, the questions contemplated, the reflections, and the varying decisions made throughout all help to craft a personal statement that stands out.

When brainstorming, use a few of these techniques for finding bits of ideas and thoughts in the corners of your brain:

- **Find a theme first.** Ask each of your three best friends to describe you in three words: two good, one bad. Keep a thick skin and tell them to be totally honest. Then assemble all of their answers and compare them to see if there's any overlap between what was said. If you notice a theme cropping up—"well organized", for example—then you should probably let the university know about this soft skill that you possess. Then reverse engineer your personal statement. Figure out an interesting way to express your organizational strength, and be sure to look at both the good and the bad sides.
- **Imitate others.** Look through examples of winning college application personal statements and see if any structures or analogies stand out to you. See if you can imitate that type of structure, or use a similar analogy, for something in your life. Note: do not commit plagiarism, which is illegal. Instead, simply draw inspiration from other people's personal statements. See the end of this chapter for some good resources.
- **Write on multiple topics.** If you have three ideas, but you can't decide between any of them, try to write a quick version of each one, no more than an hour each. In the act of

doing that, you might get inspired, or suddenly enthused, by a topic that you didn't know could be so captivating.

How to do a first draft?

The best advice you can follow is to make it sound like *you*. So leave behind the rigid formality of an academic essay, because this is not that. Toss aside the topic sentence-evidence-analysis structure that you've been learning since sixth grade. This is not that either.

First, for the first draft, give yourself permission to be bad. This is remarkably freeing. When you leave behind the imaginary expectations of the world that you think is judging you (hint: it isn't), then you can write your thoughts more freely.

Second, write more than what you need. The Common Application allows 650 words for the personal statement, maximum. A good rule of thumb is to write 900 to 1000 words for the first draft. It's always easier to pull back after going too far than it is to find yourself short a few hundred words.

Third, go too far in content. If you're not sure whether to include that sarcastic observation about the best way to level up in Fortnite, put it in anyways. You can always take it out later. Some people call this "the kitchen sink" draft, meaning you should throw in everything except that.

Fourth, some people feel more comfortable adhering to a structure, even for a first draft. If you are one of those people, try this five-paragraph format:

1. Start with a specific moment of conflict. (STORY)
2. Go back in time. Explain the background of how you got to that moment. (ESSAY)
3. Return to the moment of conflict. Show us how you got through it. (STORY)
4. Tell the reader what you learned from all of this. (ESSAY)
5. Describe the future: how this lesson will carry you through college, career, etc. (ESSAY)

Notice the denotations next to each of the five points. The first and the third paragraphs are not essays at all: they could be written like little anecdotes, pieces of storytelling. It's perfectly fine to do this. That is why this is called a personal statement, not an essay.

The second draft may need a pair of older, wiser eyes to help prune it. You could ask your parents for help, but that's not mandatory. Some students prefer to keep their personal statements hidden from their families, for many reasons. Your friends might not be the best sources of feedback either, just because most of them won't be old enough or experienced enough. And by all means, don't take advice from a college student who thinks he knows everything because he got accepted to two colleges three years ago.

Instead, the easiest and probably best thing to do is to give it to a teacher, counselor, or an administrator. If your counselor is doing a good job, he or she should be looking at it anyway. You can also use private tutors or private college counselors. Family friends who work in the field of education or media can be another good source of feedback. In short, seek out adults who are unrelated to you, and who have some experience with textual analysis. They will be your best options.

When having others proofread your essay, in addition to checking for content and grammar, make sure the reader is learning something new about you that is not easily available elsewhere in your application. Ask them to describe how they perceive you. What is it about your personality that stands out to them and makes you unique? How they answer these questions may help you to inform additional ideas and help improve your essay.

If they don't learn anything new about you from the personal statement, keep working on it. Each piece of your application must add to your overall marketing package. Recognizing that each part of the application has a specific purpose, while being mindful of each and how they build upon the next, will help you prepare a comprehensive and internally coherent application.

During my interviews with representatives from Hamilton College (Episode 102) and with Johns Hopkins University (Episode 170), both admissions representatives shared a tremendous resource available on their university websites. Called Essays That Worked, these compilations of personal statements are from students who'd been accepted, who'd written in such a way that stood out to the admissions offices. Again, these examples are made available to the public on their websites, regardless of whether you intend to apply to their schools or not.

Find both resources here:

Hamilton College, Essays That Worked: https://www.hamilton.edu/admission/apply/college-essays-that-worked
Johns Hopkins University, Essays That Worked: https://apply.jhu.edu/college-planning-guide/essays-that-worked/

CHAPTER 10
SUPPLEMENTAL ESSAYS

WHILE THE PERSONAL statement is important, there is a strong case to be made that the supplemental essays are even more crucial.

The personal statement is a single, generalized piece of writing about yourself that goes out to all colleges and universities participating in the Common Application. It isn't intended to be customized to individual schools.

The supplemental essays, however, are very much intended to be customizable. In fact, they must be.

In interviewing so many admissions officials, I have learned that writing a generic supplemental essay that can apply to any school does not enhance your overall application. This is true especially when applying to schools that are at the top of your list, where your acceptance is not guaranteed.

In fact, when admissions representatives were asked about the advice they would provide students as they sit to begin working on their supplemental essays, they spoke about the importance of doing research. Demonstrating your understanding of the school's mission, offerings, and vision, while incorporating these attributes into your own essay, will bring you a lot closer to acceptance. That's because doing so shows the admissions counselor that you understand the mission and philosophy of the university, and that you've conscientiously done your research. A supplemental essay about your past accomplishments and future plans, if aligned with the school's mission, offerings and vision, will enhance your overall application—certainly when compared with a generic essay that can be used for any school. Admissions representatives read hundreds of supplemental essays and writing one that shows you've researched their institution thoroughly can only enhance your overall application.

These supplemental questions are asked so that schools may gain more insight into the applicant, in order to determine whether the applicant is the right fit for the school.

Common types of supplemental essay questions include the following:

- **Why do you want to attend [X university]?**
- **How does [X university] align with your values?**
- **How will you use your time at [X university] to accomplish your goals?**

Oftentimes, an applicant will rush through the supplemental questions, neglecting to spend as much time on them as they did with the personal statement. This is a mistake. You should do your research. Spend time reflecting on this portion of the application.

What is really happening here is this: Admissions representatives are trying to determine your "demonstrated understanding" of their institution and how potential students see themselves as part of their community. It is vital that you do your research on the school while making it crystal-clear a) why you see yourself there, and b) how you plan on contributing to their community.

Please do not commit the cardinal sin of submitting the same supplemental essay to multiple schools by simply changing the name of the school each time. The entire point of the supplemental essay is to demonstrate your understanding of that particular school's mission, philosophy, and academic and extracurricular offerings.

Once again, you need to research the university for specific qualities that attract you.

But here's the bigger question: what to look for? You can't simply write *pretty campus* and *good food*. It's not a Caribbean resort.

Instead, focus on any of the following items—

- **Specific professors** in your field, or specific courses in your major
- **Famous alumni** who could serve as your future role models
- **Investments** that the school has made in its campus, buildings, or programs
- **Demographic data** that impressed you
- **Specific clubs** that you want to join
- **Unusual extracurricular activities** or events that pique your interest
- **People** you know who attended that university

So where do you find all this information? It's everywhere, thanks to the miracle of your web browser. Here's a starter list of places to look:

- **The university website**. Click on "news", "events", "press releases", etc. It's one of those tabs on the front page that nobody seems to ever click on. This is the place where the university boasts about all their good news. Scroll through the last two years of announcements and copy-and-paste onto your research document anything that catches your eye.
- **Google "[X University] news"**. See what comes up. This works surprisingly well.
- **Wikipedia**. While not great for academic research in history class, Wikipedia entries do contain lots of good information about colleges and universities. The reference links at the bottom of the page are very useful.
- In your chosen department, look at the **course requirements**. See if any classes look particularly interesting to you. Write

about that class in as much depth as you can, especially if it relates to your own background.
- In your chosen department, study **the professors' biographical webpages**. All of them list the professor's accomplishments and areas of research. Select the professor whose research interests coincide with your own, and write in the supplemental essay that you want to study under him or her. Just be sure that the professor isn't retired! The term *professor emeritus* usually means they've stopped teaching. [Pro tip: You can even email a professor introducing yourself before you submit an application. He or she may not respond, but it doesn't hurt to try.]
- Find **online college discussion forums** that discuss the individual universities. Read about the ones on your list. Pay attention to the contributors who evaluate the university in an even-handed manner.
- The **social media pages** of that college. This should be second nature by now.

Lastly, never underestimate the personal touch. Universities send admissions officials to college fairs all over the country, so meeting them in person doesn't have to require too much effort. If you're able to visit campus in person, that would be even better. (If you do, always be sure to register with the admissions department: they keep lists of who's been on campus.) Visiting campus not only helps you demonstrate your interest in a particular institution, but it allows you to experience so much more that is not easily replicated by researching schools online. Whether a school tracks demonstrated interest or not, take the extra step. You can write about the visit in the supplementary essay: if you had the opportunity to speak to a professor about a certain program, describe it. This would set you apart from many other applicants.

These responses don't have to be particularly difficult to write, but the research can be time-consuming. So please start the process early.

Avoid generalities at all costs. Remember, the university wants to know that you're studying it. The university wants to know that you've selected it for specific reasons. So give them those specific reasons. Furthermore, make connections between anything you've participated in throughout high school with something you witnessed at the college. Tell them explicitly how you see yourself contributing to that activity, if accepted.

That said, there are a few specific reasons for choosing a college that you should avoid mentioning, mostly because they are enormous cliches that require no effort on the part of an applicant.

- **Don't** repeat the school motto.
- **Don't** discuss how pretty the campus is.
- **Don't** gush about how much you've always wanted to live in [name of city].
- **Don't** mention its US News and World Report ranking (or any other ranking).

If you're not careful, there are many other mistakes that you can make. Ian Schachner, the admissions representative from Cornell University (episode 14), explained that if you write to him and express how you want to double major, that shows terrific ambition. The problem is that Cornell does not allow double majors across colleges. If this distinction is not made, your chances of being admitted are likely much lower.

Schachner went on to emphasize the need for original thought, as opposed to regurgitating specifics, even in the supplementary essays. "I know some applicants get advice to show the school the names of the courses that interest you most. But for a lot of our programs, we don't like that at all. We call it the Google rule. Don't put anything in your essay that just shows you can find the name of something. So if we're continuing with this theme of a marketing package, it's not about a good use of space, it's about the best use of space."

Another common mistake that students make when writing their supplemental essay, is that they neglect to answer the prompt. You could write the most eloquent essay, lacking any grammatical errors, while sounding intelligent in your choice of words and writing style. However, if you don't answer the essay prompt asked of you, it's another missed opportunity to enhance your overall application, as you neglected to address the specific question. This is why it is so important to read the essay prompt and take your time to fully understand what is being asked of you, while being mindful to answer the question thoroughly and demonstrating your understanding of the institution.

Once again, Schachner explained this well: "We select by looking at people who listen to what we said. They didn't stop at the website or the brochure. They dove deeper into the details. They are not applying to information science with what is a traditional computer science essay. They are not applying to our public policy school with what is a regular government major essay. I always say that if you really look, if you really dive into any of Cornell's marketing, our presentations, our information sessions, any conversation you have on the phone with us, we're not very subtle. We want to help people understand our unique structure."

As was the case with the personal statement, take your time, go back to it often, and edit as needed. Asking someone who will give you honest feedback to read it while understanding what is trying to be conveyed in a supplemental essay will surely help any student through the process.

Sometimes colleges list their supplemental essays as optional. However, if you're serious about applying to that school, don't view it as optional. You should still write a response and demonstrate your understanding of that institution.

CHAPTER 11
LETTERS OF RECOMMENDATION

EACH PART of the application has a general purpose, while building upon the others. The transcript shows academic ambition. The personal statement shows the applicant's voice and otherwise unknown personal qualities and beliefs. The standardized tests show an applicant's ability to thrive in a strict testing environment.

The letters of recommendation, meanwhile, serve as someone else's voice about the applicant.

Not every college or university asks for a letter of recommendation. The biggest public university system in the world, the University of California, doesn't accept them. Neither do many other large state university systems, such as Florida State University (Episode 213), Arizona State University (Episode 122), and Pennsylvania State University (Episodes 9 and 252).

But almost all private schools, and several public ones, do ask for a couple of letters of recommendation. Most typically, one is supposed to come from your high school counselor, the other from a teacher. In fact, many universities have requirements that a recommender use an institutional email address. Unfortunately, a Gmail address wouldn't be acceptable. It has to be someone who is an employee at a school. This can present a problem if you want to ask a teacher who has left the school and no longer has a functioning institutional email address.

Be mindful of who you select to write your letter of recommendation. It should be someone who knows you well from class, or from your participation in an extracurricular activity. Keep in mind though that the English teacher who gave you the A+ might not be the best person to write on your behalf, as he or she will likely talk about what a strong student you are. That has already been indicated by the grade on your transcript. Instead, consider asking a teacher in whose class you struggled a bit more. Perhaps it's the biology teacher who you had in tenth grade, in whose class you scored a little lower, but attended extra help regularly, always added to classroom conversations, and persisted despite some difficulties. This teacher will be able to give more insight into the type of student you are, your strengths, work ethic, and how you face adversity, compared to someone else who saw no struggle from you.

Don't neglect the importance of establishing strong relationships with your teachers early, so that when the time comes to ask them to write you a letter of recommendation, they are more likely to do so. I recommend asking teachers in the spring of your junior year, so that if they agree to write a letter, they will have ample notice and time to do so before applications are due. When you make the request, do so with the utmost professionalism. Approach the teacher nicely before or after class, during a moment when he or she doesn't look too busy. Have a CV in hand for them to look at, as well as a preliminary list of schools that you're going to apply to. Also be prepared to tell the teacher what your major will be, if you've decided that. Offer to send an email afterwards, and send that email the next day. Your actions during this process will continue to affect the teacher's impression of you.

Barkley Barton, associate dean for evaluation and selection at the University of Pennsylvania (Episode 166), offered some good advice about letters of recommendation. "Try to identify a teacher that knows who you are, or that person outside of the classroom who really has a sense of who you are. It's not someone that you just ran across, someone that you just met, or someone your parents just met. It should be someone who truly knows you and can really speak to your persistence, your leadership, and the impact that you've had in your high school or in your community."

Students ask me for a letter of recommendation quite often. In most cases, when students are asking me, they make an appointment to see me in person. I would recommend doing the same for whoever you ask. Don't forget to share your gratitude while expressing why you think they would be the perfect person to write on your behalf. If the teacher or administrator agrees to write the letter, that would be a good time to ask if they could write about a specific incident, initiative, or anything else that you think might add to your overall application.

It is customary to include with your request an activity sheet or resume, personal statement, and any awards or other accolades that you believe could help the teacher write a strong letter on your behalf. This can either be handed to the teacher in person or shared via email after the meeting. Provide any deadlines, special instructions, and other information related to submitting the letter. If it's been a while since you've had this teacher in class, these supplemental materials will really help him or her remember you.

Mostly, however, try to gently remind the teacher that a generic letter won't do you any good. Evidence of personal interaction with the student carries the day much further than anything else. Having a teacher solely reiterate something that is easily found on your activity sheet and/or transcript, is a missed opportunity, unless they are adding something new that enhances the overall application.

If there is something specific that happened in a classroom or a school club you participate in, don't be shy to ask the recommender to write about the specific incident if you believe it would enhance your overall application by providing new insight into who you are. You can't force a recommender to write anything specific—he or she will still choose to write about whatever he or she wishes—but it wouldn't hurt to ask. The worst that could happen is that the recommender says no. Most would say yes, especially if they agree to write on your behalf and are trying to support you through the process.

This doesn't happen often, but occasionally a teacher will agree to write a letter of recommendation, then ask the student to write it himself or herself. This is terrible. You don't want to write your own letter of recommendation, for many reasons. The first reason is that it is prohibited and constitutes fraud. The second reason is that the writing style of a high school student will not match the writing style of a teacher and could affect you negatively. The third reason is that you probably won't write as persuasively about yourself. If an overworked teacher suggests this option, politely decline and find someone else. Your future is simply too important.

The number of letters a school will accept varies based on the institution, so it is important for you to do your research for each school you are applying to, and keep organized. Using a spreadsheet to keep up with the many deadlines and details is good practice. Don't forget to thank the person writing your recommendation after the letter is submitted as maintaining strong relationships throughout the application process can only help you.

CHAPTER 12
DEMONSTRATING YOUR INTEREST

A TYPICAL QUESTION I ask the admissions representatives is this: *What are some of the things that students do to demonstrate their interest in your school, and does that demonstrated interest come into play at any point in your overall application review process?*

Whether a school reports tracking demonstrated interest, students should do so while trying to increase their chances of being accepted. With schools receiving far more applications than in previous years, thanks to streamlined processes such as the Common Application, students want colleges and their regional admissions representatives to know that they are serious about attending, with the hopes that they will increase their chances and be admitted.

There are many things that students can do to demonstrate their interest. These include—

- campus visits
- attending college fairs, either in-person or virtual
- engaging the college's admissions officers
- attending other virtual events
- signing up for a college's mailing list
- applying Early Decision

Colleges use special software that tracks whether a student opened an email. It even tells them whether the student engaged with any of the included links or not.

It is important to demonstrate interest if you intend to apply to a particular college as it will help you acquire a better understanding of what they offer students. Even if the college does not track demonstrated interest in their application review, this will help you if you are applying to a college that has a supplemental question that asks the typical question of *"why us?"*. All the things you can do to demonstrate your interest will help you better understand the academic programs, research and internship opportunities, and other possibilities available at the college. Having this knowledge will help you determine if in fact the college is the right fit for you, while helping you to demonstrate your understanding of the college when answering the supplemental essay or when speaking to an admissions representative.

Campus visits. Visiting colleges and universities is an essential part of the process. Nothing can replicate the feelings you get when you arrive on campus, and see the surrounding area to determine whether a school is the right fit or not. However, doing so can cost a lot of money, especially if the schools require long distance travel and hotel accommodations. Even if a family has the means to take such trips, finding the time to coordinate everyone's schedule due to school and work, can also be problematic, especially if you are trying to visit while classes are in session and the school is a fair distance from your home.

Many families start their college search by first visiting local colleges and universities, where long distance travel and hotel accommodations do not need to be part of the equation. Whether you intend to apply to a particular local school or not, visiting college campuses allows you to develop a feel for what you are looking for in a school such as size, location, environment, and academic offerings just to name a few. Make it a family tradition when you are on vacation to visit at least one school, even long before applications are ready to be submitted. This is a great practice to ensure that you are not waiting for junior year of high school to start the college search process, which can only benefit you and your family.

College tours aren't meant to be passive experiences. On the contrary, you should view them as your chance to actively seek answers to your questions as well as make yourself known to those who hold some power over your future.

To help, let me suggest a list of questions that you might want to consider asking when on a college tour:

- What is your student-to-faculty ratio and how will it change throughout my undergraduate years? Does this vary based on my intended major? If so, how?
- What are the housing options available to students in freshman year and beyond? Is on campus housing guaranteed for all four years? If not, what are my options? Ask to see the different housing options while on campus, especially the freshman dorms, which can sometimes be less than desirable.
- Am I permitted to have a car on campus during all my years of attendance?
- Is this a commuter school, or is it a place where most students stay on campus during the weekends?
- Can you give me an overview of your academic programs? Do you offer any 4+1 programs (bachelor's plus master's degrees) or similar options that allow students to complete their graduate degree in a shorter time? Many families consider these programs because they can reduce the overall cost of higher education.
- Is there a limit to how many Advanced Placement (AP), International Baccalaureate (IB), and/or dual enrollment courses you accept for credit? Where can I find the details to these related questions?
- What internship and/or study abroad opportunities do you provide your students, and when am I eligible to participate?

- Can I see the recreational/fitness facilities (especially if that is something that you would be interested in doing during your off time)?
- Are there police on campus and what measures does the university take to provide a safe environment for its students?
- Ask the tour guide, or even any student you meet on campus, what they wished they knew about the school before arriving, and what they would ask if they were going through the process again.

Explore the surrounding neighborhood and engage with local shopkeepers to get a sense of the community. Understanding the safety and security of the area is also important; consider researching crime statistics and asking questions about campus safety during your visit. This will help you make an informed decision about both the college and its environment.

If you are unable to visit a campus before applying, it is advisable to do so before matriculating once you receive an acceptance offer. Schools also offer multiple opportunities to conduct virtual tours and meet with admissions representatives in online meetings. If you are interested in a particular school, and can't physically be on campus, take advantage of these opportunities as they will help you throughout your search, while allowing you to learn the differences between schools.

If you want to take a guided tour, be sure to visit the school's website and register well in advance of your arrival on campus. Many schools offer self-guided tours so make sure you visit their websites well before you intend to visit. Of course, be sure to register at the admissions office so that they know you were there, and at the very least introduce yourself.

College visits are important if you are serious about attending a school. Before committing all of your time and money, physically being on campus is an experience that can't be replicated in any other fashion, especially if you are able to do so while classes are in session. While on campus, ask whatever questions you have of the students that are likely leading your tour group as a means to make some extra money on campus. If knowing what students do for fun on the weekends is important to you, ask. Don't be shy as you are not the first, and will not be the last to wonder. Remember that this is where you may spend the next four years of your life, so ask whatever questions are on your mind.

While on campus, visit and eat in their dining halls to get a taste of what they offer. If you have special dietary needs, ask what the school has to offer to accommodate. If permitted, explore the dorms and other residence halls while asking where freshmen usually reside. Oftentimes, campus tours will show you the "nicer dorms" neglecting to explain that freshmen live in other buildings that offer tighter living quarters, while having the opportunity to improve their living arrangements as the years progress. Do the dorms offer quiet study areas so that you don't have to leave the building if you want a place to study, especially at night? Visit the library, as you will likely spend a lot of time studying there, especially if there is no other quiet location to study. If athletics is important to you, visit their facilities. Is there a gym that you can exercise in using your student identification card? Is there a culture of students attending athletic events at this campus? Does that even matter to you? Consider what is important to you, and have your list ready for when you visit potential schools.

In many of the podcast episodes we acknowledged that whether it is because of cost or the time commitment, not everyone can visit each campus they apply to before submitting their application. If you don't visit before applying, you owe it to yourself to visit a school before matriculating as nothing can replicate the feelings you get when you are physically on campus, or spending time in the surrounding area, particularly when school is in session. Remember to take time to walk around campus on your own, away from the comforts of your family and try to determine if you see yourself there or not. Speak to random students and ask whatever is important to you, which may include:

- How accessible are the professors and how rigorous are the academic expectations?

- What support is available to students who might need some help with a course assignment?
- Is there a writing center or somewhere I could get someone to read one of my assignments and provide some feedback?
- What are the housing options and is on campus housing guaranteed for all 4 years
- How is the food and what options are there in terms of dining choices?
- What can you tell me about the campus culture and what do students do for fun?
- Is this a commuter school, or do most students stay on campus throughout the weekends?
- If I want to have a car on campus, is parking available for freshmen?
- What programs does the college have in place to help students transition from high school?
- What was your biggest surprise about the college that you learned about after you matriculated?
- Are there questions you wished you had asked about the college when you were doing your own research?

These of course are just some examples. Remember that the most important questions to ask are related to all the things that are most important to you.

Attending college fairs. College admissions representatives are assigned regions to cover, and they spend a significant fraction of their time visiting high schools in their territories. They also represent their institution at college fairs. All of these interactions provide students with the opportunity to demonstrate their interest while learning more about the school as part of their research to determine fit.

My advice is simple: attend the college fair and ask thoughtful questions. It is possible that a college admissions representative may remember engaging with a student, and if that student's application is in the "maybe" pile, there have been occasions when the admissions representative will advocate for that applicant's acceptance. Although this is not the main criteria for admissions into a college, letting them know that you are serious about attending their school can only help you.

Do not underestimate the benefit of following social media pages as a means to get an inside look at how active they are.

Admissions representatives enjoy talking about their school and want to help prospective students and their families through every step of the process. After a campus visit, or a virtual event, send an email to your region's admissions representative (the email address can usually be found on the school's website) and tell them your impressions. This is a nonintrusive way to let them know you are serious about their school, and may help your chances of being admitted by putting a face with your application.

In addition, attend other college fairs in your area, and be sure to introduce yourself to the representative from the schools you are considering. Letting them know that their school is on your list of top choices can only help cultivate the relationship with your regional admissions representative. There is a fine line between letting them know that you are serious about attending their school and stalking them, so be mindful of that.

Engaging with the college admissions officers. If you're going to reach out to a representative, be mindful to only do it if you have a purpose. Whether schools report that they track demonstrated interest as part of their overall application review process, they are aware when you visit campus, meet with one of their admissions counselors at a college fair, engage with any embedded email links, or attend virtual events, just to name a few. Some admissions representatives reported receiving introductory emails from prospective students before they submitted their applications. Others mentioned hearing from students who had recently visited campus to share their observations and specific aspects they appreciated about the school.

Schools increasingly receive applications from more viable candidates to admit than they have seats available, but it can still help you to demonstrate your interest. This is particularly true when someone is waitlisted or deferred, a method schools use to see how many accepted students will actually attend before offering additional seats, as determining the percentage of accepted students that will actually attend (yield) has become more challenging. If waitlisted or deferred, don't wait for the college to provide their final decision. Reach out by email and explain that you will attend if accepted, and provide anything new that may not be in your application, including any leadership initiatives, recognitions, or your senior year grades. In many cases, colleges will ask you to accept your position on their waitlist. Be sure to closely follow the directions that the college provides. Often, you will be asked to indicate on their portal that you are interested in remaining on their waitlist. Make up your mind quickly: colleges can see the length of time between your opening the email and selecting this option on their portal. That length of time may affect your chances of being promoted off the wait list.

On my podcast, many admissions representatives have encouraged sending them emails with questions. It is important to ask a thoughtful question not easily found on their website, to demonstrate that you're doing your research and are writing about something really specific. Perhaps it could be something related to your intended course of study or specific to other programs the college offers. Remember to do so with a specific purpose, as you certainly do not want to present yourself as too pushy. Find the right balance.

During my interview with the admissions representatives from Oberlin College and Conservatory (Episode 217), they spoke about how they do not offer a supplementary essay asking "Why Oberlin?" as many other schools do However, they spoke about how, if deferred, a student may want to reach out and express his or her continued interest, while submitting a detailed account as to why he or she wants to attend their college.

Meanwhile, Rick Clark, the assistant vice provost and executive director of admissions at Georgia Tech (episode 200), emphasized the need for applicants to ask big-picture questions about the institutions they're applying to. "For students, the biggest and most important thing is that kids need to feel more empowered to ask the questions that they care about and what matters to them. Think about your own high school and all of these college reps that come to visit. It's a great question to ask, hey, what are you trying to achieve at your school? What are your institutional priorities? That's not a taboo question, that's a great question."

More to the point, asking questions and building relationships with the admissions representatives can lead to one of them standing up for you at the moment when it counts the most: the decision to admit. Evan Sprinkle, the dean of undergraduate admissions at Elon College (Episode 220), said, "We always encourage students to come visit campus. And then once that visit happens, the following steps are really about building a relationship with your admissions counselor, right? Because that person is going to be the student's advocate through this process, when we sit down as an admissions committee to make final decisions on files. It would be my job to advocate for students from my territory. I would say, *I'm excited to present John to you. Here's what I've learned about John academically. And here's what I also know to be true about how he will engage as a student in the campus community.* And so it's really important to maintain those relationships with your admissions counselor as well, because they're a big important voice for you. So that campus visit is an important part of starting that relationship."

During the process of demonstrating your interest with all the methods listed above, you should be learning about the academic programs the school offers, opportunities available outside of the classroom (such as study abroad options and internships), and other details of the community. It is very helpful, in a supplemental essay, or when being interviewed by a school where they offer such an option, to be able to articulate why you see yourself on their campus, which specific program you'd like to enter, and what aspects of their school community appeal to you. On the flip side, you should also let them know how you see yourself contributing to all of those communities. So whether or not a school tracks demonstrated interest as part of their application review process, it doesn't really matter as taking all these steps will help you regardless.

CHAPTER 13
APPLICATION TYPES

FORTUNATELY, the college applications process in the United States isn't quite as messy and decentralized as it was twenty years ago. But it could still be better. Some countries, such as the United Kingdom, have a central application website, a single channel through which almost everyone submits their applications.

We don't have that. Instead, we have a small tapestry of different applications. You may need to do one, two, three, possibly even four or more different application forms in your process, depending on how widely you cast your net.

Let's take a look at all the options.

THE COMMON APPLICATION

commonapp.org

This is the most popular tool for college applications in the United States. It features over 1000 member colleges and universities in the U.S., plus a few more in Canada, China, and Europe. Many of those member schools use it as their only application portal, so the chances are that you'll probably need to use it.

The Common App is a nonprofit whose mission is to push for equity, integrity, and greater access in the application process. It's been a lifesaver for many and makes applying to a large number of colleges as easy as possible.

The site opens for new signups each year on August 1. When you open an account, you will be able to see the prompts for the personal statement, which largely stay the same each year. The personal statement written on the Common App is used universally and sent to all member universities. As you add individual colleges and universities, you can see the supplemental questions where applicable, which were discussed earlier. Those tend to take the most time, especially for the selective schools, so be sure to start the process early.

The home page features five tabs: Dashboard, My Colleges, Common App, College Search, and Financial Aid. To select a school, go to College Search and type in the name of the school and click *add*. Now the school will appear in your My Colleges tab. The colleges and universities release their supplemental writing questions and other supplemental requirements at various times throughout the year, some sooner and some later. You can start preparing your supplemental responses whenever you can see them, so be sure to add the schools that you're interested in as soon as possible.

To fill out the main part of the application, the part that will be sent to all colleges and universities, just click on the Common App tab. You'll see a vertical menu on the left: Profile, Family, Education, Testing, Activities, Writing, and Courses & Grades. You can fill out each of these sections anytime. It is recommended to get it finished before September of your senior year, so you don't have to think about it during the fall semester.

- Under **Family**, in addition to basic biographical data, you'll have to answer whether you have children. Many applicants come from nontraditional backgrounds.
- Under **Education**, you'll have to provide a list of your fall classes for your senior year. You may not be able to provide

this until September, if your schedule doesn't get finalized until then.
- Under **Testing**, remember that it is not mandatory to submit standardized tests to schools that are test optional or test blind. However, if you decide to report your standardized test scores, please follow up by sending official SAT/ACT score reports as well. For those who decide to submit test scores, an official record is mandatory. The best thing to do is to send the test scores on the same day that you send the applications. The schools will attach them to your application as they are received.
- Under **Activities**, you'll need to list all your extracurricular activities. Be sure to put them in rough order of importance, which means putting the most meaningful, time-intensive one first, and then the next ones in decreasing order of importance. After that, include your position or role, the name of the organization, and a brief description. Please note: The description should not repeat the position. Try writing the description by beginning with the verb, like this: *Organized annual fundraisers, traveled to tournaments, and recruited new members.* The rule of three works well here, meaning the use of parallel structure with three verbs. The last entries are hours per week and weeks per year, and it's fine to estimate those.
- Under **Writing**, there is a tab called Additional Information. This is an open box, with 650 words at your disposal, to write about anything you'd like. It's advisable to use this for really important things, like explaining a sick parent, your own illness, a death in the family, a divorce, a severe financial difficulty, or even the fact that you're a twin. (That's no joke: if you're a twin, both of you should put that fact in the additional information. Colleges like to admit twins together. It's a small boost.) If you choose to write something here, just be sure that it's informative.
- Finally, under **Courses & Grades**, some colleges require you to add all your courses and grades to the application.

Basically, they want you to copy your entire transcript. Triple check your work: college admissions officials track your reported grades against your real transcript, so if you've made a mistake, it could cost you.

The Financial Aid tab gives you a brief outline of the options you have for affording college, including grants, scholarships, loans, and work-study programs.

THE UNIVERSITY OF CALIFORNIA

https://apply.universityofcalifornia.edu/my-application/login

The University of California is the largest public university system in the world. In 2023, it received a quarter of a million applications for first-year and transfer admissions. It is the 800-lb gorilla of college admissions, and it is so large that it maintains its own robust application system.

The University of California (UC) system generally does not accept letters of recommendation and does not require standardized tests (SAT or ACT) for admission. Currently, a UC application primarily requires three elements: your grades, your extracurricular activities, and your personal insight questions. However, admission policies can change, so it is always good practice to check the university's website for the most up-to-date information.

Instead of a single personal statement, the UC system provides eight personal insight writing prompts, and asks all applicants to respond to four of them. The responses are limited to 350 words each, which means that you'll be doing a maximum of 1400 words of writing.

The prompts stay remarkably consistent from year to year. Here are the eight prompts, as of 2024.

1. *Describe an example of your leadership experience in which you have*

positively influenced others, helped resolve disputes or contributed to group efforts over time.

2. Every person has a creative side, and it can be expressed in many ways: problem solving, original and innovative thinking, and artistically, to name a few. Describe how you express your creative side.

3. What would you say is your greatest talent or skill? How have you developed and demonstrated that talent over time?

4. Describe how you have taken advantage of a significant educational opportunity or worked to overcome an educational barrier you have faced.

5. Describe the most significant challenge you have faced and the steps you have taken to overcome this challenge. How has this challenge affected your academic achievement?

6. Think about an academic subject that inspires you. Describe how you have furthered this interest inside and/or outside of the classroom.

7. What have you done to make your school or your community a better place?

8. Beyond what has already been shared in your application, what do you believe makes you stand out as a strong candidate for admissions to the University of California?

Efficient applicants will use their personal statement for the Common Application as one of their four personal insight responses, in a shortened form.

The UC application opens on August 1 each year, and the application deadline for all 10 UC campuses is November 30. You can apply to as many campuses as you'd like with the same application, but each campus charges an $80 application fee. So, for instance, if you apply to three UC campuses, you'll need to pay $240.

You'll need to input all your grades manually, the same as you'll need to do for certain colleges on the Common Application.

The university will eventually compare your inputted grades with your official transcript, later in the year. Unlike many other colleges and universities, the UC system does not require your transcript at the time of application. It can be sent much later, after you're admitted: the final deadline is July 1 in the summer after your senior year.

The application provides spaces for up to 20 activities and awards, but don't feel panicked if you can't fill all the spaces. Almost nobody can. Remember that the best applicants have just a handful of extracurriculars that they've done for several years: depth of commitment is really what impresses admissions committees, not sheer number of activities.

Please scan the QR code below to access the list of podcast episodes featuring interviews with UC schools and more:

THE STATE UNIVERSITY OF NEW YORK

https://www.suny.edu/

As a proud product of the SUNY system and a New Yorker myself, I'd be remiss not to include the SUNY application, which, like the UC system, allows students to apply to multiple campuses across the state with a single application. This makes it an attractive option for both in-state and out-of-state students. While out-of-state students may face higher tuition rates, as is the case with most state schools, the SUNY system offers a wide variety of academic programs and campuses to explore. Given its importance in my own educational journey, I wanted to ensure this option is highlighted for students considering schools in New York.

Please scan the QR code below to access the list of podcast episodes featuring interviews with SUNY schools and more:

THE COALITION APPLICATION

https://www.coalitionforcollegeaccess.org/

Founded in 2015, the Coalition App is intended to assist disadvantaged students. Approximately 170 member schools currently accept it. It actively works with colleges to offer fee waivers to students who cannot afford them.

Unlike the Common App, it features something called "the locker", which is an online storage space where applicants can place projects, essays, photo albums, or anything else that they want admissions representatives to consider in addition to their application.

Though the Coalition App is viewed as equal to the Common App, a limited number of schools are affiliated with it. Check its list against your own list. It may cost extra effort to use the Coalition App if you will also need to use the Common App.

INDIVIDUAL APPLICATIONS

Though most small and private universities have chosen to use the Common Application, a few have opted to keep their own individual online applications. Other than the University of California system, these include the California State University system, Massachusetts Institute of Technology (MIT), and Georgetown University, plus many religious and military institutions of higher learning that have unique applicant pools. Some schools don't use the Common App simply because they enjoy putting up an extra layer of difficulty to ensure that only the most motivated applicants will apply. Consult these school's deadlines at the beginning of senior year: some are remarkably early.

CHAPTER 14
APPLICATION DEADLINES

THROUGHOUT MY INTERVIEWS with the college admissions representatives, they shared their knowledge of various application types, deadlines, and in some cases whether there was any benefit to applying one way over the other.

Note: More than a few of them spoke about the importance of staying organized, since application types and deadlines vary by institution. It's hard to keep up with the constant changes. One way to organize yourself is to open a spreadsheet, perhaps a Google Sheet or an Excel doc, and track yourself that way. There are other methods: use whichever one works best for you. Checking a school's website for the latest guidelines is always a recommended part of the college admissions process.

Let's take a look at the various types of application deadlines. There is a lot of misinformation and misinterpretations floating around regarding this part of the process, so please read this chapter carefully.

Here's a quick summary of each one.

EARLY DECISION (ED) 1

November 1 is the most common ED deadline. Applying ED is a binding agreement. If a student applies Early Decision and is accepted, that student *must* attend that school. Since it is a binding agreement, <u>he or she may only apply Early Decision to one school</u>, clearly indicating that this school is the first choice over all others. It's the best way to demonstrate your interest in a school and an excellent choice for those students who have a very clear and obvious program that they're aiming for. After all, some students have known, ever since they were quite young, that University of X is the only place for them. However, ED doesn't always mix well with other components of the admissions process. For example, students may need merit aid money to afford a certain university, but merit aid money decisions are typically awarded in April—nearly five months after ED acceptances are sent out! And students aren't permitted to give a conditional acceptance based on future scholarship money or financial aid. This paradox prevents many students from applying for ED.

Some misguided students think they can circumvent the system and back out of an ED acceptance because they're not legally enforceable, but that's not advised. It's important to approach this process with integrity, and to play the game according to the rules. It's really difficult for admissions officers to know who is genuine in their acceptance, and recall that estimating "yield" is one of the difficult parts of the admission process. Not attending a school that accepted you for ED will carry overall negative consequences.

Applying Early Decision is a very serious thing, and you need to make absolutely sure it is the correct decision for you. Once you've passed through that door, assume there is no walking back.

That said, there are a few instances when a student could legitimately back out: for instance, for a severe family illness. On other occasions, a small percentage of ED acceptances cannot come to a financial aid agreement with the university that accepted them, and will ask politely to be released. Admissions committees will sometimes avoid accepting ED applicants who have these types of potential issues. The process is flexible, and students should communicate with college admissions officials to find out what compromises can be made.

EARLY DECISION (ED) 2

Like Early Decision, this is also a binding agreement, but with a later deadline. Generally, students who apply ED2 are those who weren't ready to do so on November 1, but are ready to do so by the end of December. Sometimes these are students who were denied acceptance to their first-choice ED school, and so they are now trying again by committing to a different school for ED2. Sometimes the students were waiting on additional accomplishments. Sometimes they were trying to enhance their transcript by waiting for first-semester senior year grades to be released. Like ED, students may only apply to one program for ED2.

EARLY ACTION (EA)

Unlike ED, this type of application is non-binding. It has an early application deadline, typically by mid-November. Applying EA also allows students to receive admissions decisions earlier. I would recommend applying EA to all schools that offer it. This is partly to get all applications in by the November deadline, which frees up students to enjoy their senior year of high school while waiting for the admissions decisions to come in. Unlike applying ED, applying EA doesn't obligate students to attend any of the schools that offer acceptance. Furthermore, students may apply to as many EA schools as they wish, and they will be able to compare financial aid packages between schools where they are accepted.

RESTRICTIVE EARLY ACTION (REA) OR SINGLE CHOICE EARLY ACTION (SCEA)

This is non-binding and similar to Early Action, except it is typically used by more competitive private colleges and comes with restrictions. Typically, students can't apply in the same manner to other private institutions. If students apply Restrictive Early Action or Single Choice Early Action to a private institution, they may still apply Early Action to public or international schools, as they are not obligated to attend a college that may accept them under Restrictive Early Action/Single Choice Early Action. Applying in this manner demonstrates to a private institution that a student is serious about their school, but of course it does not guarantee admission. Please note that it is very important to check the individual school policies for those who wish to apply Restrictive Early Action or Single Choice Early Action, to ensure compliance.

―――――

REGULAR DECISION

RD generally has a later application deadline than the previous types of applications, thus providing students more time to prepare their overall packages. Regular Decision is a non-binding decision and students are able to compare offers from the multiple schools where they received acceptances. One of the benefits of applying Regular Decision is that first-semester senior year grades will almost always be available for students to submit. So if students feel that they will demonstrate an upward trend in their performance academically during senior year, they may apply Regular Decision to include mid-year senior year grades, which will hopefully help with their overall application. It is very important to stay organized and check the deadlines for each of the colleges you are applying to, while ensuring that you are not missing anything important.

―――――

ROLLING ADMISSIONS

RA is a process whereby schools evaluate applications as they are received, usually leading to a quick turnaround in terms of an admissions decision. Penn State University (Episodes 9 and 233), for instance, opens its Rolling Admissions application each year on August 1, and the process continues throughout the year until all spots are filled. It is always beneficial to submit your application as early as possible if you are applying for Rolling Admissions, to better your chances of not being denied because all of the spots were filled. Penn State University reported beginning their rolling admissions application review as soon as they start receiving applications on August 1, while other schools such as Louisiana State University (Episode 178) stated that although their rolling admissions application opens on August 1, they don't start evaluating until a few months later.

CHAPTER 15
THE ROLE OF A COLLEGE ADMISSIONS OFFICIAL

FROM AUGUST TO DECEMBER, college admissions officials spend a lot of time traveling. They're out seeing their territory that they've been assigned, trying to meet as many people as possible via recruiting. It's not unusual for a college admissions official to visit four high schools in a single day, if they're located close to one another.

Those high school visits can be a lunchroom visit under a banner bearing the name of their university, chatting with anybody who stops by. Other high school visits might be more targeted, with specific interviews or chats scheduled with various potential applicants in private offices or empty classrooms. They can also spend time at alumni events, meetings with prospective parents, college fairs, and even meetings with entire groups of high school counselors to answer high-level professional questions.

By November, in what little free time they have, the admissions officials will begin to read applications, beginning with early decision, then proceeding to early action, and then eventually to regular decision. The reading period extends all the way until the beginning of April, and officials take breaks periodically to conduct informative sessions for applicants visiting campus. Other admissions officials work from home two or three days a week, reading applications for eight to ten hours at a time.

This is why you want to craft a unique personal statement. Your application will be sitting in an electronic stack of 50 to 100 other personal statements that, unfairly or not, your own will be judged against.

Other admissions officials, the ones who work with athletes, have different schedules. They juggle meetings with potential recruits, visit games or matches, field phone calls and emails from parents, and shoulder the reading portion of the job as well.

Sometimes the head of the admissions department will mandate a weekly "ad comm" day, meaning a day when all admissions staff must come into the office. On these days there will be full staff meetings, check-ins with supervisors, discussions of borderline applicants that are not clear admits or reject, and many phone calls facilitating the arrival of applicants' transcripts. At large colleges, the admissions staff is split into a group of readers—who mostly just read applications at home—and a group of visitor services specialists who meet with the applicants and their families.

Based on my 250+ podcast interviews, I have my own set of observations of college admissions representatives. A few of these insights I've already shared, but I repeat them here because they're important.

First, it came up quite often in our conversations that they are admissions officers, not rejection officers. In other words, they are looking for reasons to admit you. It is up to the student to submit a comprehensive college application that presents them in the best possible light, while ensuring that each piece builds upon the next. The officials stressed that this application should not repeat information. This makes their jobs easier, and you definitely want to make it easier for an admissions committee to select you.

Furthermore, it was very common for the admissions representatives to explain their application review as being holistic. They looked at academic and non-academic factors to help them determine whether a student would be admitted, waitlisted, deferred or rejected. This was a constant refrain I heard from them, which means that you can probably stop worrying about that C you earned in ninth grade.

The first thing that an admissions officer will look for is whether you are able to handle the academic challenges of their institution. To do so, they will look at your transcript to see what courses you took, based on the context of what was available to you in your high school, while reviewing how you performed. Past academic performance is the best indicator of how you will perform once in college. If test scores are available, they will also use them as part of their holistic review process to determine if you can handle the academic challenges.

Remember that admissions representatives have looked at thousands of applications. After a couple of years on the job, they have developed a keen eye for the type of transcript that they know will work. Sometimes they use shorthand with one another to describe applicants. LMO, for instance, means *Like Many Others*.

It's best not to end up as an LMO.

Aside from academics, admissions representatives want to know the type of community member you will be, the type of roommate or classmate you will be. They look for the things that you will participate in once on their campus and the ways that you will contribute to the overall school community. So the admissions committee will look at what you participated in outside of the classroom while in high school, keeping in mind (note this, once again) that quality is far more important than quantity. Being part of a few clubs, where you showed initiative and took on leadership roles is perceived as better than having a laundry list of clubs with not much for you to share in terms of your participation.

Admissions representatives often emphasize the value of highlighting significant personal responsibilities you have undertaken during high school. These responsibilities could include part-time work to contribute to household expenses or caring for younger siblings or elderly family members. Such experiences can demonstrate important skills such as leadership, time management, and personal dedication. They also provide context for any gaps in extracurricular involvement. Without this context, admissions officers might speculate about your activities or interests, potentially leading to assumptions that may not accurately reflect your experiences or capabilities. Presenting a comprehensive view of your responsibilities and how they have shaped your high school experience can contribute positively to the holistic review of your application.

A typical question I ask on the podcast episodes is whether the admissions representatives use the GPA as indicated on the transcript, or if they recalculate it using their own metrics. Many reported recalculating the GPA, since high schools do not have a standard way in terms of how they evaluate students. Some use numeric grades, others use alpha. Some weigh advanced courses, while others don't offer any or have far less.

In short, high schools are so different that GPAs are often recalculated and many admissions representatives reported that when they perform their calculations, their main focus is on the core academic subjects including science, mathematics, English, social studies, and world language. Admissions representatives from schools such as Emory (Episodes 6 and 211) and Carnegie Mellon (Episodes 47 and 208) reported to me that, though they can see all grades available on a student's transcript, and use them as part of their holistic review, they only use grades 10 and 11 when recalculating the students' GPA as part of their process.

Territory plays a role too. Admissions officials are distributed by territory, and their job is to learn about and establish relationships with all the high schools in a particular area. Erica Woods, senior associate director of admissions at Villanova University (Episode 202), said, "Students think that we want students from a specific type of high school, but the reality is we want the best students from every high school. And this is where the professionalism and the expertise of the territory counselors comes into play. So just for context, my territory is New York City, Long Island, Philadelphia, and Louisiana. What that means is I am charged with keeping up to date with the schools within my area. It's my responsibility to understand the differences between this school and that school, what their grading scales are like. We take all of these things into account when we're evaluating a student. And that is why it's so important for us to review our territory applications so that we can give that context."

I found one other final type of answer while making my podcast. It became clear in the episodes that what they are really looking for in a supplemental essay, which is not necessarily found in other parts of your application, is your demonstrated understanding of the institution. They want to know why you see yourself on their campus, and how you plan on contributing while there. This is where all the research you've done, and all the effort that you've made to demonstrate interest, can help you. It doesn't even matter if they know about all this research and effort either. The result will be clear in your supplemental essays, when you show them just how well you understand their school.

CHAPTER 16
COLLEGE ADMISSIONS INTERVIEWS

STUDENTS SOMETIMES BECOME fearful thinking about the possibility of being called to a college admissions interview. An interview is not something to be afraid of. In fact, you should welcome an interview as a chance to shine.

First, understand that college admissions representatives explain that there are two types of interviews: informative and evaluative.

- In an **informative** interview, you are meeting with someone in the admissions office to provide you with additional information about the college.
- In an **evaluative** interview, you are being interviewed as part of your overall application process.

Whether a school claims that the interview is for informative purposes only, or evaluative in nature, it's always advisable to assume that you are being looked at to see if you are going to be a good fit for their school. But this is also a two-way street. As part of the interview process, you should also be looking to see if the school is the right fit for you, and you should take the time to ask questions that are important to you.

While it's true that interviews help admissions committees understand a student better, they sometimes have more specific purposes. Some interviews are meant to assist an applicant with academic and career planning. Many art, design, and performance schools hold interviews to review and discuss portfolios.

For instance, Berklee College of Music posts its admissions interview questions online. It places strong emphasis upon the 15-minute interview, as much as it does upon the audition. In fact, a great interview, at that school, can make up for a mediocre audition, since not everybody who attends a music college is planning to be a performer. Likewise, at certain art colleges, interviews are informally conducted *before* an applicant submits a portfolio, just to make sure that the portfolio is complete—and also to make sure that the applicant knows what he or she is getting into. It doesn't do any good for a budding young visual artist who creates avant-garde contemporary graphic design to apply to a program known for its old-school study of human anatomy. So this is a function that an interview can serve as well, as part of the screening process.

Religious universities use interviews for different purposes, depending on the institution. Mildly religious institutions, like College of the Holy Cross, often suggest that applicants schedule an interview. Other religious universities, such as Yeshiva University, make interviews mandatory. These schools look at the depth of religious belief of their applicants, and for evidence of dedication to a community filled with said religious beliefs. Fairfield University (Episodes 20 and 235), a Catholic Jesuit school, does not require any interviews at all.

In general, the more unique the college or university, the more likely it is to insist upon an interview. Deep Springs College, for instance, is a school that few people have heard of, and yet it is more exclusive than some of the most famous Ivy League schools. Deep Springs is a junior college—two years only—with a grand total of 26 students. It is located inside a working cattle ranch high in the mountains on the border of Nevada and California. Tuition is free, and after two years the students transfer to big-name selective universities. In a tiny place like that, you can understand how important admissions interviews can be. The administration uses them to screen closely.

Likewise, St. John's College (Episode 222), which runs a very well-known interdisciplinary Great Books program, requires two admissions interviews: one with an admissions counselor, and one with a faculty member. These are conducted for much the same reason. Personal statements are only 650 words, so a 20-minute interview can tell them as much if not more about the applicant.

Some universities with high numbers of applicants may offer interviews with alumni who typically live in the same area as the applicant. This type of interview often feels less intense than an interview with an admissions official on campus.

Some schools not only offer these types of interviews, but basically require them. For other schools, they are optional and barely regarded. For all of them, however, you'll likely meet the interviewer at a place convenient to both the interviewer and yourself. It could be at the person's office, at a cafe, at a bookstore, at a public park, etc. Some of the alumni will treat it more formally, while others may show up in sandals and t-shirts holding their young children by the hand.

Wherever it takes place, remember to take the interview as seriously as any other. What you say in the interview may either support or corroborate what your application and recommendations say, and that may help your cause. While these interviews don't necessarily carry the same weight as an interview with an admission official, the alumnus does write a report about your chat and will send it to the admissions office. At times, especially when faced with many applicants who have similar credentials, the admissions committee will turn to those alumni interview reports for a fuller picture of the individuals. It is impossible to say whether they can be deciding factors: that insight is usually only known to the admissions committee.

But it is worth your best try.

In preparation for your interview, be sure to research. Be ready to explain why you are interested in this particular school. If it is because of the majors or the minors the school offers, be ready to articulate why you want to pursue a degree in that program, while being well versed in the school's offerings. If there are professors you've learned about that you want to work with, do your research and make sure that they are still active members of the school community, not retired. Talk about your visit to campus; perhaps you knew as soon as you arrived that this is where you want to spend the next four years of your life and explain why. Was it the community, internship opportunities, research initiatives, programs of study or a combination? Be prepared to articulate your why.

At the end of the conversation, when they ask if you have any questions, make sure you do. You can prepare some final questions ahead of time. At the very least, you can turn the question back on them, asking what it is about their college or university that they love so much. You could get some new information this way.

Most of all, be authentic. This is easy to say but hard to execute in practice. It means that your words must match your demeanor, your body language, and your background. Here are a few things that can help you establish authenticity:

- **Eye contact.** Eye contact is frequently cited as one of the behavioral traits most linked with trustworthiness. But there is a limit to it. Hold eye contact too long, and you'll give off some vibes that make people uneasy. There is a middle ground, and practice it until you feel it. You can sometimes begin a thought by looking up in the corner of the room, then eventually bringing your eyes down to the other person's eyes when you deliver the main thrust of a thought.
- **Openness and conscientiousness**. On the famous chart of the big five personality traits, these are the two that colleges typically prize the most. (The other three are extraversion, agreeableness, and neuroticism.) It would be to your advantage to display your openness and your conscientiousness during the interview. You can transmit openness by discussing your passion for learning new things

or having new experiences, and then providing specific examples of those academic and extracurricular activities on their campus. Conscientiousness is defined as being responsible, careful, and diligent. This can be displayed during an interview by bringing up examples from your life when you showed diligence, or relating anecdotes that indicate a need for order and organization.

- **Future-time orientation**. One of the things that defines life in the United States—and many successful people in the United States—is our ability to project ourselves, mentally, into a bigger, better future. In fact, many of the most dynamic cultures in the world have this same mentality. So colleges often look for this quality in applicants, especially schools that pride themselves on creating young professionals. You can display this in the interview by discussing your goals for the future. Pro tip: Some of your responses should use the verbs *will*, *would like to*, or *plan to*.
- **Confident responses.** Demonstrating confidence in your responses is crucial. This confidence is strengthened by providing focused answers and staying composed, even if faced with interruptions or unexpected questions. While it's unlikely you will encounter intentional disruptions in a university interview, being prepared to handle any unforeseen circumstances gracefully will reflect positively on you. Remember, showing poise and the ability to remain on track can significantly enhance your interview performance.

Finally, when you're finished, be sure to send a thank you card. Buy a card, write it by hand using ink, and be sure to send it by snail mail either the same day of the interview or the day after. In today's digital age, receiving a handwritten thank you note is rare. Such a personal touch can make a memorable impression, while possibly helping you to stand out in the admissions process.

Many interviewers, especially the admissions officials, have a stock series of questions that they like to ask the applicants. It would be good for you to know what they are, so that you can prepare your answers in advance.

What follows is a list of the most common ones. Make sure that you have rehearsed your responses to all of these questions:

- Tell me about yourself.
- How did you hear about our school?
- Why do you want to come to this school?
- Why do you want to study your specific major?
- What are your academic strengths that you will bring to our program?
- What are your academic weaknesses? How have you addressed them?
- What achievement are you most proud of?
- What does being successful look like to you?
- In the classroom, what type of student are you?
- What do you plan to bring to this school?
- Who do you most admire?
- What's the last book you read? What are you reading at the moment?
- What do you like to do for fun?
- What is an obstacle you've faced and how did you get through it?
- Describe yourself in three adjectives.
- Where do you see yourself in 5 years?
- What do you think about [recent current event]?
- If you had to describe your role within your family or friend group, what would it be?
- Do you have any questions for me?

The first thing to do is to copy these questions onto a word processing program of your choice (Google Docs, Microsoft Word, etc.) and answer them in writing. Do this just for yourself. If you plan early, you will have days, weeks, even months to think of good answers.

If you're having trouble with making a response, take it to an adult in your life. It could be a parent, it could be another family member, it could be a teacher, it could be a counselor, it could be a neighbor. Be sure it's someone whose opinion you respect, and likely someone who works in a professional, collaborative environment. You know the type of person I'm referring to. They should have good social skills and some awareness of how to present themselves to others. Ask that person for help formulating the response.

Once you're satisfied with the responses, practice saying them to yourself. You don't need to look in a mirror: that won't help much. Just walk around your room, your house, your neighborhood, saying your answers to yourself until they eventually become second nature.

Next, record yourself speaking those answers. Listen back to your own responses too. Pay attention to unusual gaps, weird vocal tics, awkward pauses, etc. Be ruthless, and pretend like you're analyzing someone else's performance. A friend who is good at debate or forensics might be useful as a sounding board in this situation.

Finally, ask someone to help you rehearse, ideally the same adult as before. Parents might not be the best choice here; it's best to get yourself out of your comfort zone, and parents could disrupt you in unnecessary ways. Ask the adult to ask you each question on the list. Answer them the best you can, using no notes. Write down what the adult tells you should be changed about each response.

Asking people for help is key. This shouldn't be a solitary pursuit. You should ask for support. After all, you're a teen, and this is one of your first introductions to the world of adults.

A word about body language: Be aware of it. The best position for your body is with feet flat on the floor, pointed towards your interviewer. You should either be sitting straight up or leaning slightly forward. Your hands should be visible, so place them on the table, folded. If there is no table, just put them on your thighs. You can also lean forward slightly and place your forearms on your thighs and let your hands dangle between your knees. Your abdominal muscles should be slightly tense. After all, this is an important moment. You can use some hand gestures to emphasize your points, but if it doesn't feel natural, don't bother.

Anxiety is a common issue, so some deep breathing can help you prior to the interview. There are many online forums, such as Reddit, that can help you relieve some of your anxiety too. Read about other people's experiences with college interviews, and it might help you to calm down.

CHAPTER 17
APPLICATION RESPONSES

THERE ARE four major types of responses you can receive from a college or university: **acceptance**, **rejection**, **waitlisted**, or **deferral**. Let's look at what each one means.

ACCEPTANCE

This is the response everybody dreams of. You can often see the online result in whatever portal you use to apply, but you'll also get a paper acceptance packet in the mail a few days or weeks later. Early Decision and Early Action applicants will get the letter in December. Regular decision applicants will typically get this letter in the first week of April.

Holding that in your hands makes it feel official. The letter usually gets straight to the point, in the first sentence: *Congratulations! We are delighted to inform you that you have been admitted to…* Or: *It is with great pleasure that we offer you admission to…*

After that, you'll typically see a few sentences complimenting you and your hard work in high school. This usually includes a discussion about how competitive the applicant pool was this year and how proud you should feel of yourself. Then the letter usually goes into some logistical items, and it always sets a deadline to respond (usually May 1).

This is undoubtedly the best part of the process. You should feel a huge sense of relief when you get these letters, even from safety schools. My advice is that you keep them somewhere safe. Years later, you may want to dig them out and look at them.

In the meantime, begin to keep track of all the offers of acceptance on your spreadsheet. If you haven't made one yet, this is the perfect time. Make columns for acceptance deadlines, housing options and costs, meal plans, financial aid offers, and anything else you decide is important. Once you decide upon the winner, be sure to send in the required deposit before the deadline so that you don't lose your spot! The deposit tends to be anywhere from 100 to 500 dollars.

Also remember that once you send in that deposit to your chosen university, you also need to decline acceptance at all the other schools.

―――

REJECTION

As with acceptances, you will find out about your rejection first from the portal that you used to apply. However, you'll also receive notice in snail mail. It will be a disappointingly thin letter, a single piece of paper folded over three times. Usually it begins with a comment about the massive number of applicants the school has received that year. The letter usually then moves onto the regretful news that they simply cannot accept all the qualified applicants. And then they deliver the death blow that, unfortunately, you are one of the people who cannot be offered admission.

This is disappointing, but remember that if you're not getting rejections, you're probably not selecting colleges correctly earlier in the process. In other words, most of your reach schools (typically all of them) should reject you, as should some of your target schools. Challenging yourself by applying to schools that are potentially a little bit out of your range will by nature result in rejections. Embrace it. You only need one acceptance anyways.

If it's your top-choice school that has rejected you, it's okay to feel disappointed for a while. But remember that just because a school is your top choice doesn't mean that you are its top choice. I'll go over some of the many reasons for rejections in an upcoming chapter. Most of them have little to do with you.

There are a lot of urban myths about applicants who came up with inventive ways to sneak their way into an acceptance. One of the best is the legend of the applicant who sent a letter that rejected the rejection, and informed the university that he would be attending class that fall. This makes a fun story, but it doesn't work, so please don't try it.

There are legitimate ways to appeal a rejection, but it's quite unusual for a college to flip its own rejection. Their decision is final in more than 99 percent of all cases. However, there could be a situation that you believe warrants a second look, especially for first-choice schools. If so, you can write a letter of appeal, which must contain new information or demonstrate extenuating circumstances that weren't found in your initial application. An important new award (think Science Olympiad), an athletic achievement (set a new school record for goals scored in lacrosse), or a new diagnosis for an ill sibling whose mysterious behavior had distracted you in the first semester of senior year—all of these are legitimate things to bring up. It should also repeat your stated belief that the school is your first choice.

However, I'd point out that after receiving a rejection is the wrong time to write this letter. These extenuating circumstances should be revealed to the college or university earlier in the spring, before they make their admission decision, not afterwards. I'd also emphasize the fact, once again, that *any communication you make with the admissions department must contain new information about you.* If you write a generic letter repeating everything that you've included in the application, you'll be seen as a pest, and it could hurt your chances of acceptance. So if nothing has changed in your life, there is no need to contact them, and there is no reason to appeal the rejection.

WAITLISTED

This is the purgatory of the college application process. If you find yourself waitlisted, it means that you have been neither accepted nor rejected.

If this happens to you, don't get down on yourself. In fact, remember that this could mean that you've qualified for acceptance, but the school most likely doesn't have room for you at that moment. The admissions office is waiting to see how many of its offers of acceptance will be turned down by the other applicants. At that point, once it finds out its yield, it will be able to extend an offer of acceptance to you.

Here are some numbers to help you understand what the colleges are dealing with. According to NACAC (the National Association for College Admissions Counseling), the average yield rate for a four-year college is currently about 30 percent. It's slightly higher for private schools (33 percent) and slightly lower for public state universities (25 percent). Remember that yield is the percentage of admitted students who enroll at an institution. If you get accepted at four different schools, for example, you can only accept at one of them. Turning down the other three will affect those schools' yields.

The bad news is that, in recent decades, colleges have become much better at estimating their yield. In the distant past, the estimates were more wildly off, and schools would sometimes extend offers of acceptance to a large percentage of the waitlist. Today, however, they often use some pretty sophisticated software and have teams of really bright statisticians to help them with this estimation. For this reason, it has become overall more difficult to get off the waitlist into an acceptance.

Today, the average percentage of students admitted from a waitlist is currently about 20 percent. For the most highly selective colleges, that number comes down to about 7 percent. The University of Pennsylvania (Episode 166), which is a highly selective Ivy League school, accepted only 40 of the 2288 students on its waitlist in the 2023-2024 admission cycle. That's less than 2 percent.

There are many reasons why an applicant could be placed on the waitlist. Here are a few of them:

- **They don't have enough room.** Colleges are limited by the number of beds on campus and the number of seats in the classrooms. They simply can't admit everybody who is qualified, which is why it is recommended to apply to multiple target schools.
- **You had some flaws.** Nobody is perfect, and some colleges will care more about that C in honors chemistry than other colleges do. They may also waitlist if your academic credentials are stellar, but you had few if any extracurricular activities and couldn't account for any of your non-academic time.
- **You were too strong a candidate.** It's true. Sometimes colleges look at your curriculum, your GPA, your activities, your letters of recommendation, and think, *Wow, this young lady is way too qualified for our school. She would never accept here. Better to waitlist.* There is nothing that can be done about this, unfortunately. They are selecting you as much as you are selecting them.
- **You applied for a very competitive major.** This happens a lot to applicants in the performing arts and in computer science. If there are too many applicants in one area of study, the admissions office will put several of them on ice (meaning the waitlist) while it attempts to create a more balanced class from a wide variety of majors.
- **Your parents are important.** If your family members are big donors, or if they're well-connected at the school, the admissions office may decide to waitlist you rather than reject you outright. This is considered a common courtesy for some legacy applicants who don't measure up to the academic requirements.

Remember that not every university has a waitlist. In fact, less than half of them do. Also remember that if you are offered a place on a waitlist, you don't have to take it. It's okay to turn down the school at that point, if you have your eye on a better offer elsewhere.

However, there is one possible situation that is tricky to resolve.

This occurs when an applicant is waitlisted by his or her reach school while at the same time being accepted by a top target school. A risk-taker might wait for the dream school to respond. However, most people who are wise and cautious would accept at the target school instead. The reason is that admissions officials don't typically begin going through the waitlist until late May. But National College Decision Day is May 1, the deadline for accepting admission at almost all colleges and universities. If you decide to gamble with your future and forfeit a deposit at any school, including your target school, then your only move is to wait for the reach school to make up its mind. You will have missed decision day, the target college will slip through your fingers, and you could very well end up going to no college at all, if the reach school doesn't admit you from the waitlist. Remember how low those percentages are.

It's ultimately your decision, but I see no reason to mess around with your future. A reach school isn't worth missing freshman year.

So if you are waitlisted, is there anything that you can do to improve your chances of admission? Absolutely there is. First, contact the admissions office and ask if they rank the people on the waitlist. Some schools do, some don't. If they do, then politely ask if they wouldn't mind telling you where you sit on that ranking. If they agree, then use that information and act accordingly.

Second, you can conduct a gentle but insistent full-court press to make your case to the admissions office that you deserve an offer of acceptance. Follow up by email immediately after being waitlisted, and then stay in touch at least every few weeks with additional information about yourself. You can tell them about new accomplishments or awards as you continue to earn them, in the second semester of your senior year. Think of this, again, as a marketing campaign. But keep the follow-ups short.

The whole purpose is to stay on the radar of the admissions officials so that, when they begin handing out additional acceptances, your name and continuous demonstrated interest are at the front of their minds.

As you're trying to navigate these decisions, know that the majority of schools have what is called a Common Data Set, which one can easily search for online. (Just search for "common data set University of Michigan", for example.) The Common Data Set provides a lot of relevant data about a school, including the percentage of students who were accepted, percent who were rejected, and the percent who were waitlisted. It also reveals the percent who ultimately attended, along with many more insights to help students and their families gain more clarity into the college admissions process.

―――――

DEFERRED

Sometimes students are deferred from their Early Decision or Early Action colleges. However, *deferred* does not mean denied. In the words of Rick Clark, admissions representative at Georgia Tech (Episode 92): "Well, we like to joke a lot about the idea that it's too bad that deferred and denied both start with *de-*, because they are very different. A deferral means *tell us more*. It's a maybe, a hold on." And Kaitlyn Marshall at the University of Miami (Episode 36) says, "It's simply a pause on the application. We'll come back to it, we'll review later—that is all it is. It's not a closed door."

Often, the college needs additional information before it can make a final decision, so the admissions office moves the student's application into their regular decision round. Perhaps they need to know how many students will accept their offer from their early rounds. Maybe they want to see the caliber of applicants in their Regular Decision round before making a final decision.

If students are deferred by a school that they wish to attend, they should let their intentions be known. When deferring an applicant, colleges and universities usually ask if that applicant still wants to be considered for admission. If so, indicate *yes*, usually on a question in the application portal. As one would do for a waitlisted decision, if anything new of significance happened since submitting the application, such as a recently-won award or a new accomplishment, let the admissions office know.

Sara Cohen, associate dean of admissions at the University of Pennsylvania (Episode 166), agreed. "If you'd like to indicate your continued interest in Penn after being either deferred or waitlisted, we invite you to submit just one update to us, anything. It could be a short letter that you'd like to add about your involvements or your activities since submitting your application, plus anything else you'd like to say about your continued interest in Penn. And one letter is just fine. You do not need to submit multiple letters or other materials to us."

FINANCIAL AID AWARD

For applicants who've received acceptance, and if they've indicated that they are seeking financial aid, another letter typically arrives on the heels of the acceptance packet. That is the financial aid award letter, which indicates how much financial aid the school is willing to offer. It will contain information about federal loans, scholarships, grants, and work-study programs. The exact timing of its arrival depends on the submission of the FAFSA as well as the university's particular administrative process.

This letter is usually of greater interest to the applicant's parents than to the applicant, but the applicant should not underestimate its impact. If a college or university cannot offer enough financial aid to an applicant, or if a different college or university offers a better financial aid package, then the applicant may decide to turn down the first school, regardless of its position on the applicant's personal ranking.

Also, remember that financial aid letters are only for one year each. You need to resubmit FAFSA every year to determine the aid that you're eligible for, and you'll get a new financial aid award letter a few months later.

CHAPTER 18
THE TEN MOST COMMON TYPES OF FOUR-YEAR COLLEGES AND UNIVERSITIES

WHEN STUDYING a large group of anything, it's helpful to know the individual categories or demographics that are contained inside the group. The same goes for colleges and universities. In this chapter, I'll describe the ten most common types of four-year institutions of higher education in the United States.

THE BIG 10

Say the words Big 10, and most people immediately picture a football game inside a huge stadium. But the real definition of this group is a bit more nuanced.

Yes, it's true that the Big 10 is a group of universities that belong to one of the most well-known collegiate athletic conferences in the country. However, despite what its name suggests, the conference actually consists of 18 colleges. These schools are large institutions that have a tremendous amount of school spirit, expressed through athletics and other ways. They are located primarily in the upper Midwest, though four West Coast universities have been recently added.

They are also major research universities with huge financial endowments and well-known academic reputations. All of them enroll over 20,000 students, and a few of them over 40,000 students. In short, they are the powerhouses of higher education.

Yet overall they're not highly selective. Most have acceptance rates somewhere in the 50 percent range. One outlier in the group is Northwestern (Episode 257, and the only private school in the Big 10), which has an acceptance rate of 7 percent. Michigan State University (Episode 7), on the other hand, has an acceptance rate of 88 percent.

If you're applying to these schools, recognize that they do carry some drawbacks. You'll most likely be experiencing harsh winter weather, which some people cannot tolerate. Also, many of those schools are not geographically diverse: they pull primarily from the state in which they're located. After all, those students take advantage of cheap in-state tuition: as of 2024, in-state tuition at the University of Michigan (Episode 12) is only $17,000 per year, but out-of-state tuition is over $60,000 per year.

So the student body may not be as diverse as they will be elsewhere. Most significantly, the size of the general requirement classes will be enormous, up to 200 people each. If you're looking for personalized instruction and professors who know your name, this is a bad fit.

LAND-GRANT UNIVERSITIES

The Morrill Acts of the 1860s established a series of state colleges whose mission was primarily to educate students in agricultural, mechanical, and military pursuits. This was unusual at the time, when a college education typically meant studying Greek and Latin, or history and poetry. The intention was to guarantee a strong engine that generated enough food and machines to drive forward the rapidly urbanizing and industrializing U.S. population. It turned out that these schools did exactly that. Some historians cite the land-grant schools as one of the primary reasons why the United States became a superpower in the twentieth century.

Today, most of those land-grant colleges have become reclassified as land-grant universities. There are over 100 now, at least one in every state, and many are solid choices, such as Purdue University (Episodes 74 and 263) in Indiana. Some may surprise you: both Cornell and MIT (Massachusetts Institute of Technology) are land-grant universities.

Like the Big 10, land-grant universities have large populations and low tuition. They have huge introductory classes and even bigger football games. They also receive large amounts of federal funding for research, along with matching state funds. For this reason, they are good choices for anyone looking at the fields that they were originally intended for a century and a half ago: agriculture and engineering. For instance, the best dairy science program in the United States is at the University of Wisconsin (Episode 155), a land-grant university. At Cornell, the engineering department has been its flagship program for longer than all of us have been alive, and it is still the most respected engineering program in the entire Ivy League. However, students serious about the liberal arts would probably be better off avoiding these types of schools and selecting a small liberal arts college instead, cost permitting.

Many of them do have caps on the numbers of out-of-state students that they are permitted to take. Jason McGrath, associate provost and director of undergraduate admissions at UNC-Chapel Hill (Episode 199), commented: "At Carolina, we have an obligation as a state institution that 82% of our incoming first year students are North Carolina residents, and only 18% can be non-residents. There's actually institutionally financial penalties if you don't hit those numbers more than one year in a row."

LIBERAL ARTS COLLEGES

Some people view a liberal arts college as a small place where privileged students avoid learning useful things and indulge in esoteric subjects. This is not accurate. Liberal arts colleges teach one important thing, above all else: critical thinking.

Liberal arts colleges are four-year undergraduate institutions that offer degrees in humanities, sciences, and social sciences. It's purposefully broad, and a liberal arts degree emphasizes soft skills such as writing proficiency, analytical thinking, clear communication, and leadership ability.

Liberal arts colleges have small campuses and even smaller classes, with typically no more than 20 students per class and 2000 students total. They are often smaller than many public high schools. They are private institutions, not public, and they receive very little research funding from anywhere. For these reasons, tuition tends to be quite expensive, though most students receive merit-based financial aid. They rarely offer graduate degrees.

Most importantly, because of the small class size, students typically build strong relationships with their professors. It's not uncommon to be invited by a professor to a coffee shop to discuss a particularly thorny academic or intellectual problem. For students thinking strategically about their future, these experiences provide a better opportunity to earn a top-level letter of recommendation for graduate school. Many students choose liberal arts colleges to prepare them for medical school, law school, and other professional graduate programs.

At these schools, you'll know everybody in your class, for better or for worse. There is no anonymity, and this can be a drawback, depending on your point of view. Also, without research opportunities, students interested in, say, chemistry will need to step outside the college to find laboratory internships and other scientific work. Many liberal arts colleges suffer from lack of name recognition. Most are located in small towns in the Midwest or the East Coast.

They do punch above their weight, though. For instance, Harvey Mudd College in California boasts one of the most highly-rated math programs in the country, and it only has 900 students.

Critics do point to one issue with liberal arts colleges: their lack of specialization. After all, these schools do graduate well-educated critical thinkers who nonetheless lack specific skills that some (not all) employers look for. That can be an issue for those who are seeking concrete specialized employment immediately after college, but it brings up a related problem that people have been debating for centuries: is the purpose of higher education to prepare its graduates for the workforce? Or is it to create critical thinkers who have the mental flexibility to survive in a rapidly changing work environment? Liberal arts colleges believe in the latter.

THE IVY LEAGUE

Its fame is so great that its very name has come to serve as a shorthand for privilege and excellence in the United States. The words *Ivy League* dazzle a lot of people, and its graduates include many of the most powerful people in the world. Once upon a time, centuries ago, this group of schools were among the very few in the United States to offer a great education, but today there is a lot of competition from many other schools that are perceived as either equal or better.

The eight schools that make up the Ivy League are Brown, Columbia, Cornell, Dartmouth, Harvard, UPenn, Princeton, and Yale. They have every possible benefit known to an institution of higher education: centuries-old traditions, enormous financial endowments, huge research opportunities, great academic coursework, exciting classroom discussions, extensive alumni networks, world-renowned faculty who often have written the textbooks that are used in their classes, and much more.

In order to guarantee all that excellence, the Ivy League intentionally limits its acceptances. Most have 5 percent acceptance rates right now, and many have admitted that they could admit a much larger freshman class without reducing the quality of their student body. But they maintain a firm circle of exclusivity, which has paid off very well for them.

There are a few drawbacks to the Ivy League, including extremely high tuition costs. Certain students with enormous self-importance have been surprised to find themselves surrounded by many other people who are just as intelligent as they are, which disappoints them and can sour their experience. Students often report highly competitive classrooms and study environments. Later in life, some Ivy League graduates find themselves judged harshly by non-Ivy League graduates, and as a result feel the need to conceal their university history. For Harvard graduates, revealing their Harvard background is even known as "dropping the H-bomb".

But fortunately, it isn't 1905 anymore. The Ivy League is not the only place to receive an excellent education, as you've already seen in this chapter. In fact, there's a whole additional class of schools called the Ivy Plus, a category that is subdivided into the Public Ivies, Little Ivies, and more. These schools offer the same (or better) education and research opportunities as the eight members of the Ivy League. The bad news: they're often just as exclusive. These schools include the University of Chicago, Stanford, Duke (Episodes 86 and 256), Johns Hopkins (Episode 170), and others.

For all applicants, the Ivy League (and the Ivy Plus schools) are reaches. Nobody is guaranteed entry there, and they reject nearly all of their applicants, including many excellent ones. If you're one of the people who've decided to shoot their shot at the prestigious name schools, the good news is that there are over 4000 other colleges and universities willing to accept you.

TECH SCHOOLS

The increase of the industrial power of the United States after World War II led directly to the growth of the tech schools. They are dedicated to engineering, science, math, and technology. In other words, these schools are pure STEM, though most of them do have some required basic courses in liberal arts.

All of them have some variation of the word *tech* in their names: Colorado Technical University, Florida Polytechnic University, Michigan Technological University, etc. Some, like MIT (Massachusetts Institute of Technology) are immensely rigorous, while others are somewhat less demanding of their students.

For those applicants who are born knowing that they have a future in technology and engineering, these are excellent choices. Applicants who are tentative about entering the STEM field may want to apply to a similar program at a non-tech university, in case they decide to transfer to something else completely.

Keep in mind also that a four-year technological university is different from a two-year tech college. A technological university offers a broader STEM education and grants a Bachelor of Science degree. A tech college prepares its students for narrow and specialized careers in things like automotive maintenance technology, dental hygiene, HVAC repair, etc. They are practical and focused solely on future employment.

SINGLE-SEX SCHOOLS

They still exist, just like single-sex high schools still do. But their numbers have fallen. In the 1960s, there were over 250 four-year women's colleges in the United States. Today, that number is 26. The men's colleges have fallen even further: there are only four men's colleges left in the entire country. Most of these schools went coeducational partly out of principle, and partly out of need for tuition.

There are still some advantages to single-sex education. Girls in a single-sex classroom often display a higher level of confidence in their ability to learn and perform in STEM subjects than do girls in a co-ed classroom. This effect is very pronounced at the high school level, and it continues at the college level as well. There is less gender stereotyping, and the environment tends to be more academic without the distractions provided by the opposite sex.

Today, there are many co-ed private liberal arts colleges that only recently started admitting men in the last few decades. Goucher College (Episode 191), for instance, is a small liberal arts school in Baltimore that was a women's college for a full century until 1986. Goucher still hasn't achieved equality in its acceptance gender ratio: it is currently 67 percent female, and 33 percent male. These schools often seek out male applicants in their quest to balance their gender ratio, so take note.

RELIGIOUS-AFFILIATED SCHOOLS

This category is larger than you may think: there are 849 religious-affiliated schools in the United States. They are mostly Christian schools, with a few Jewish and Mormon ones as well. Some are religious in name only, having mostly outgrown their distant religious roots. Georgetown University, for example, is not anyone's idea of a religious school, given its strong political and international reputation, but it remains a Jesuit Catholic school. At the other end of the spectrum, some religious-affiliated schools are religious from head to toe, with strict rules about behavior and religious observance.

Something that may be surprising to people is the fact that religious-affiliated schools are often open to applicants who do not share that religion. They often ask for the applicant's faith during the admissions process, but how much weight is placed upon that response varies between schools. The schools are often hungry for more tuition dollars; many like to present themselves to non-believers as open, universal, and nonjudgmental institutions. The Catholic University of America in Washington, D.C., for example, is the only university in the United States that operates directly under a papal charter. Yet 20 percent of its undergraduate students are not Catholic at all: many are commuter students from the surrounding neighborhoods of the city. In fact, some religious institutions even draw strong believers of different faiths, because of the applicants' perception that living in a religious environment (any religion) is preferable to a non-religious environment.

Academically, there is often no difference between a religious school and a non-religious one. Sometimes, a simple theology course or two is required, but even those can sometimes be substituted with general ethics classes. Most religious classes are not driven by religious agendas, but instead offer classes that explore diverse viewpoints. It is common to find professors offering classes in world religions, the problem of evil, and even contemporary topics. Very few religious-affiliated colleges or universities require extensive theological coursework. The class sizes tend to remain under 20 students, which can be another attractive quality.

THE HBCU SYSTEM

Our system of HBCUs (historically black colleges and universities) schools was founded in the late nineteenth century, most of them in the years after the Emancipation Proclamation was issued. About 90 percent of them are found in the South, for obvious historical reasons, and there are about 100 total. The most famous, Howard University, is often called "the black Harvard", and Morehouse and Spelman also enjoy name recognition. Just as religious institutions are open to non-believers, so too are HBCUs open to non-black applicants. In fact, the overall number of non-black students enrolled at HBCUs has been climbing, from 15 percent in 1976 to 23 percent in 2022. Nearly 70 percent of HBCU graduates are female, highlighting the same shift towards a female-dominated undergraduate population that has been seen across all of higher education.

By far, the biggest reason that students attend an HBCU is for the deep sense of shared culture and connection with other black students, plus an academic community that examines the entirety of the American experience. However, HBCUs also tend to be more affordable than their counterparts. Several studies have shown that graduates of HBCUs enjoy a greater sense of well-being than non-HBCU graduates do, and they tend to build more successful professional careers than non-HBCU graduates do.

On the other hand, HBCUs often lack research money and facilities that are available at many other types of schools, and their alumni networks may be smaller, since they are limited primarily to the black community. Often, their influence is felt most strongly in the region surrounding the school, so graduates who leave the region will often find that the name recognition of their school is not as well-known elsewhere.

SERVICE ACADEMIES

The five major military academies are West Point, Naval Academy, Air Force Academy, Coast Guard Academy, and Merchant Marine Academy. Each one has a unique affiliation with a different branch of the U.S. military: West Point, for example, is affiliated with the U.S. Army. The only branch of the military that doesn't have its own dedicated service academy is the Marine Corps. The Naval Academy is the only possible route into the Marines, since the Marines began as a branch of the U.S. Navy nearly two hundred years ago.

The service academies aim to do more than just educate academically. They build strong minds, strong bodies, and strong characters. At these institutions, the tuition is completely free, funded by the federal government, and may even include a small stipend. The environments are very strict, as you would imagine at a military college. And military service is mandatory after graduation; remember, these academies are trying to train future military officers.

The requirements for the service academies are quite different from any other type of institution of higher education. They demand the usual high GPA and high SAT scores (math is weighted more heavily than reading and writing). They ask for letters of recommendation and demonstration of leadership potential. However, they require a medical exam, a difficult fitness test, and a congressional nomination (except the Coast Guard Academy). It is a long process that should begin well before the January application deadline. In fact, passing the fitness exam alone may take months of physical training.

These schools are not for everybody. They require a lot of discipline and immense commitment to a greater cause. Plebe year (freshman year) can be very emotionally difficult. If you decide to leave, you may be asked to repay the government for the tuition you used. The choice of classes isn't as extensive as you will find at other schools. And the multi-year military service after graduation is mandatory; you may find yourself assigned to a war zone halfway around the world, with no way out.

But the extensive alumni network and the prestige that comes with graduation from these institutions are undeniable. As a part of the experience, you will get the opportunity to travel the world a bit and undertake some incredible physical training exercises in amphibious assault, mountain climbing, and other areas. The heat and intensity of the college experience will shape you and your outlook for the rest of your life, perhaps more than any other category of school in this chapter.

ART COLLEGES

On the other side of the spectrum from military academies lay the nearly 300 accredited art colleges of the United States. These are schools that foster individual creative expression through the use of precise and well-established techniques. Some can be very free-form and *laissez-faire*, while others can be traditional and strict.

Art colleges have drawbacks, of course. Some of the instructors won't have any professional experience in art, only academic experience. This can be a problem for those who are training for a job. Regarding employment, a college degree in art doesn't matter nearly as much as a strong portfolio does. Therefore, it is technically possible to skip college altogether, if you can figure out how to improve your skills to a professional level. Some students decide that the expense of art school isn't worth the effort, and leave in order to educate themselves using online videos. This is possible but not recommended, except for the very few who are mature and disciplined enough to give themselves an entire college education.

After all, an art college carries you through a well-tested curriculum that forces you to learn what you didn't realize that you needed to know. It teaches the importance of meeting deadlines and following instructions. It offers studio equipment that you may not have the ability to afford. And networking is always a boon, both with classmates and with professors.

It is always possible to attend a regular university and major in fine arts. Almost all the selective schools have a fine arts department, including Carnegie-Mellon, the University of Michigan, Northeastern, and many others.

When applying to any art college or art department, one mandatory part of the process is to build a good portfolio of work in a variety of styles. This cannot be done overnight, or in two weeks: it should be begun long before senior year. Then, be sure to take advantage of National Portfolio Day, when counselors, admissions representatives, and professors from accredited art schools offer free portfolio reviews to interested applicants.

CHAPTER 19
INTERNATIONAL APPLICANTS

THE AMERICAN SYSTEM of higher education is one of the jewels of the world, though it is easy to forget that for those of us lucky enough to be born here. There are 46 million immigrants currently living in the United States (out of a population of 330 million people), and a good number of them came here for education, either for themselves or their children.

The number of international students has been growing for decades. In 2003, there were just over 570,000 of them. Twenty years later, by 2023, that number had increased to over 1,000,000. About half of those are from either India or China, the two most populous countries on earth. The most popular majors continue to be in the STEM fields, with math and computer science (23 percent) and engineering (19 percent) making up nearly half of all international applicants' majors.

The international students who decide to stay in the U.S. often become integral parts of our multiethnic society. One out of every five people who begin start-ups in the United States is an immigrant, and a majority of them initially came to the country for college. The ones who decide to return to their home countries carry with them the training that they received here. In fact, there is no country on earth that has trained more foreign heads of state than the United States.

But international applicants face a huge array of extra obstacles that they need to overcome just to get to the stage of the process that U.S. applicants find themselves in right from the start.

Let's take a look at a few of the extra challenges that international applicants face.

- **Mandatory language tests.** International students are usually required to submit a language test proving their fluency in English, even those who went to an English-language international school. There are three exams that can be taken: the TOEFL (Test of English as a Foreign Language), IELTS (International English Language Testing System), or Duolingo. TOEFL is most widely accepted in the US, IELTS is most popular in the UK and Australia, and Duolingo is the new kid on the block, racing to steal business from the other two.
- **SAT.** While a test-optional admission policy sounds great from the outside, international applicants often feel more pressure to submit scores simply because they want to provide more familiar data to the admissions committee. It's almost done out of reassurance. The problem is that scoring highly on the SAT isn't as easy for international students as it is for U.S. students. For students who don't speak English as their first language, reading comprehension, vocabulary, and grammar can present much more difficulty. Plus, the exam isn't as neutral as you might think. Our standardized tests, as much as we'd like to believe are culturally sensitive, do carry deeply embedded cultural markers. These questions ask students to express their intelligence in ways that they've never been asked before, and the adjustment is jarring. Math word problems, for example, are rarely asked in certain cultures, and students from those areas become frustrated at having to parse sentences instead of performing math.
- **Extracurricular activities.** In foreign countries, there often aren't many specifically-designated extracurricular activities

for high school students. Some high schools will even purposefully oppose extracurricular activities, because they view them as distractions from the business of pure academic learning. In the Middle East, female students often fight an uphill battle to be permitted to start or even join an after-school club. As a result, many international applicants have shorter activities lists than U.S. applicants have.

- **Transcripts.** There are countless types of school grading systems across the world. International applicants who've attended international schools with American curriculum abroad don't have a problem in the application process, but a student who's attended a local high school in a foreign country is facing a potential problem in this department. University admissions committees do their best, but they don't always understand every grading system they are presented with. Furthermore, all academic transcripts in foreign languages must be translated by a credentialed and certified translation service.
- **Letters of recommendation.** Teachers and administrators in foreign high schools often do not understand the importance of letters of recommendation. Many times, they don't live in a culture that values those types of letters. Or, if they are valued, those letters tend to be impersonally written, which does no good whatsoever. In the worst-case scenario, the teacher or administrator asks the foreign student to write his or her own letter of recommendation. This can happen because they don't know the high value that a U.S. university places upon it. It can also happen because the adult doesn't know English, in which case there are accredited translators who can translate the letters into English. All of these problems happen more often than you think.
- **F-1 visa.** This is the well-known international student visa, and applying for it can take up to two months. It can be denied on many grounds, including suspicion that the student intends to stay in the U.S. after graduation. The visa,

once granted, prohibits international students from working off campus during their first year at school. Beginning in the second year, the student is permitted a maximum of 20 hours of work per week. Even obtaining the visa requires proof of funds to sponsor your education and living expenses during your stay. Proving this can be daunting for international students from modest backgrounds.
- **No federal financial aid.** International students obviously don't qualify for any federal or state financial aid, period. Universities can provide their own financial aid, mostly through scholarships, but most of that money is limited to graduate students. Overall, most international undergraduate students must pay full price.

Because of all this, international applicants often come from wealthier families, and the ones who successfully win acceptance to the U.S. often begin preparing for their journey years in advance.

There are still other problems. Exchange rates can fluctuate a lot, depending on the country, and they're normally not important for U.S. applicants. But many international applicants plan to pay for college with their family money, typically kept in local currency. This means that, if the local currency tanks, some applicants see the price tag of their education skyrocket. In that situation, many choose to give up their dreams.

Finally, many cities are poorly organized around the world, especially in places like Latin America and Asia. This can present problems with transportation and crime, problems that Americans are unfortunately familiar with as well. These things can also affect a student's transcript, as a series of cascading events outside of the student's control can lead, for example, to one or two failed classes. That, in turn, can affect the student's application. These problems definitely can be found in the United States as well, but they exist to an even greater degree in the developing world. International applicants are well advised to utilize the additional information box on their Common Application forms to explain these types of external problems that may have affected their academic performance or extracurricular activities.

For the international applicants who make it through this obstacle course, they then encounter restrictions on the percentage of international students who are accepted each year. At Dartmouth University, for example, that number is 15 percent. The number at UNC-Chapel Hill hovers quite a bit lower, around 6 percent. Meanwhile, NYU might have the highest percentage of international students in the country: 22 percent.

Universities have to walk a very thin tightrope when deciding how many international students to admit. They have many factors to consider. For private schools heavily dependent upon tuition, one undeniable factor is the fact that many international applicants pay full sticker price for their education. This is very attractive from a budgetary perspective. On the other hand, state universities that run primarily on public money also face strict rules about serving their state applicants first, and everyone else second. That is quite understandable as well.

Unfortunately, the attractiveness of the United States as an education destination has begun to wane a little bit. During the covid-19 pandemic, the USCIS (United States Citizen and Immigration Services) stopped issuing student visas for a while, which sent international application numbers plummeting. As of 2024, that number has mostly recovered.

But there are two systemic problems that are beginning to drive international applicants away:

- The skyrocketing cost of tuition.
- The foreign perception of gun violence in the United States.

Both of these trends are causing some international applicants to turn to the UK or to Europe for college. We shouldn't let that trend continue. American society will only benefit by continuing to attract talented and motivated students from other countries.

Finally, let me leave this chapter with some interesting statistics about international students in the United States.

- About 28 percent of all tuition money paid to colleges and universities comes from international students. They have been viewed as a cash cow by our higher education system for a very long time. They pay about three times as much tuition at public universities as do U.S. citizens.
- China has sent more students to the U.S. than any other country. In 2019, there were about 370,000 Chinese students enrolled in U.S. institutions of higher education. That number has fallen a bit lately: in 2024, it was down to 290,000. This reflects the declining state of U.S.-China relations and was accelerated by the mysterious origin of the covid-19 pandemic.
- The number of international students from India is rising fast and will likely exceed the number of international students from China in 2024.
- Foreign students are two to eight times more likely to cheat on exams than are American students. This could be because the stakes are much higher for international students than for U.S. students. It could also be a byproduct of the intensely academic cultures of China and South Korea that place heavy and unforgiving emphasis upon academic performance.

CHAPTER 20
FOR-PROFIT HIGHER EDUCATION

MOST OF THE schools discussed in my podcast, and in this book, have been non-profit or public schools. However, there is an alternate universe of schooling: the for-profit world of higher education.

It has been criticized lately because of some very bad predatory practices that some of these schools have practiced. However, for-profit schools have brought educational opportunities to students in a way that makes them more accessible and convenient, allowing people who otherwise might not be able to obtain a college degree to complete their studies while working, raising a family, or handling other responsibilities that come with life as an adult.

It might be good to start with a bit of historical context. For-profit educational institutions have existed for hundreds of years. The earliest examples can be seen in colonial-era America, where entrepreneurs taught skills and trades (along with reading and writing) in their homes, charging students fees for these services. Many of these teachers were clergy who needed money to supplement the small stipends they earned running their churches. Sometimes, their wives even joined in to teach sewing, weaving, and other things that would one day be called home economics.

Major historical figures, such as Benjamin Franklin, dismissed the classics-heavy curriculum of "proper" schools like Harvard. Instead, they encouraged the growth, on a parallel track, of institutions of entrepreneurial education. From their earliest days, these for-profit schools (sometimes known as career colleges) taught skills like navigation, surveying, and other subjects linked to the country's economic growth. Later, those subjects grew to include new trades such as bookkeeping, engineering, and technical drawing. The tech colleges, discussed in the previous chapter, are a continuation of this tradition.

Today, a for-profit college prioritizes making money off its students. Funded by investors, these schools take the tuition and fees and return the profits to the pockets of those investors: their first concern is themselves, not the student-clients. Since 2018, for instance, the principal investor of DeVry University has been Palm Ventures, a family investment firm, which attempted to reclassify DeVry as a nonprofit university in order to avoid a multimillion-dollar annual tax bill. For-profit schools primarily offer technical, trade, and vocational certification programs, though a few offer bachelor's degrees and master's degrees as well.

The demographics of students at for-profit colleges and universities on average is older than the demographics of students at four-year colleges and universities. Sixty-five percent are over the age of 25. The students are mostly women, around 70 percent or so. For-profit schools also have a high percentage of veterans as students, since there are loans available for individuals who've served in the military. There are additional demographic trends: these students are more likely to be from minority groups (22 percent are black), and they also report lower incomes than students at public and not-for-profit institutions. Significantly, they also report lower levels of previous education, with many less likely to have graduated from high school. Overall, for-profit schools have become places that provide educational opportunities for people often defined as disadvantaged or marginalized.

As a result, these students have different expectations of a college experience. In the eternal battle between whether education should enlighten minds or train workers for jobs, this population is on the side of practical, skills-based learning. These students often can neither afford nor want classes in, for example, the history of medieval Italy. Instead, they enroll for one reason: to succeed in society through career advancement. They want to equip themselves for the marketplace, and the for-profit sector does this better than many traditional paths.

The for-profit sector was booming in the 1990s and 2000s, thanks to the success of schools such as the University of Phoenix. From 1995 to 2010, total enrollment more than tripled. The sector boasted about its role as the future of higher education.

But the sector has quite a few problems.

There are a lot of similarities in the overall goals of for-profit schools and their public and not-for-profit counterparts. Both kinds of educational institutions—in fact, *all* kinds of colleges and universities—are affected in similar ways by external forces such as economic cycles, student demographics, market demands, loan programs, regulatory environments, and financial subsidies forced on them by government agencies.

And for-profit colleges have some undeniable benefits. With the ability to pivot quickly, the business model of for-profit educational institutions is more responsive to the needs of the economy than the public or not-for-profit model. A rapid change in workplace demands can translate quickly to a change in curriculum, which can result in jobs in high-demand fields that pay good salaries. It's quite easy to win acceptance at a for-profit school, since it has a strong interest in admitting as many students as possible.

The scheduling of classes is often made to suit the lifestyles of its students, many of whom work during the day. The for-profit sector has always developed and relied upon different methods of distance learning, with Penn Foster conducting the first correspondence classes by postal mail in the mid-1800s. More recently, this sector was the first to move into online classes in the 2010s, while the four-year universities were very slow to catch up, reluctantly forced to do so by the covid-19 pandemic.

But recently, its problems have become severe.

For-profit colleges don't have proper regional accreditation, only national accreditation. But regional accreditation carries much more rigorous standards, including recognition by the U.S. Department of Education. For that reason, the education that is provided at these schools tends to pale in comparison with the education received at a nonprofit or public four-year college or university. This is especially hard to swallow given the price tag: tuition at a for-profit school can often run higher than in-state tuition to a four-year public university. The student debt that is generated by these schools is very significant, and it doesn't necessarily match the level of the education.

Even more worrisome, these schools close very abruptly, and with little notice. When I say *abruptly*, I mean that very literally—students show up to class only to find the building is locked. In many cases, it's same-day closures. This is happening all over the sector. Approximately 80 percent of the schools that closed from 2004 to 2020 were for-profit schools. From 2020 to 2024, the covid-19 pandemic obliterated many more, affecting nearly 50,000 students, nearly half of whom never bothered to return to any classes anywhere. Another complication is that, because these schools lack regional accreditation, students cannot transfer their credits to other institutions. This leaves those students completely out of luck.

The biggest black mark against the for-profit sector is the way that the sector has exhibited fraudulent business practices. In 2021, the Department of Education issued $1.1 billion in loan forgiveness to the 115,000 students who'd taken out loans to attend the defunct ITT Technical Institute, which had abruptly closed its doors in 2016 after years of hiding its true financial state. This left many without a path to finish their studies. The next year, in 2022, the Department of Education discharged another $4 billion in loans for students at the same school.

See, the for-profit model doesn't care much about graduation rates, except where government oversight forces it to do so. Traditional four-year colleges and universities, on the other hand, have a vested interest in making sure everybody graduates.

The value of the degrees from these schools is very questionable, specifically the bachelor's degrees. Some employers won't consider an applicant with a degree from a for-profit school.

Given all of these problems, it is almost always a better choice to attend a traditional four-year college or university. The biggest argument for attending a for-profit school these days is the way it caters to busy working adults via distance learning, online classes, and classes held at nights and weekends. But the risks are just too big. Cost-wise, it will often be slightly cheaper to attend an in-state public university. Even earning an associate's degree at a local community college is a better choice than paying for this type of education, at least until the sector stops closing schools so suddenly and possibly swindling students.

CHAPTER 21
ASSESSING YOUR APPLICATION PROFILE

IN MY PODCAST, admissions representatives have used the word *holistic* literally hundreds of times to describe their decision-making process. That means that they look at every element of your application and make their final decision according to what they sense about your profile overall.

But is that helpful? Aren't there at least some metrics these admissions representatives use to judge applications? When they're sitting around the table making their decisions about applicants, what sort of things do the admissions officials really talk about?

Let's look at a few of those ways that an application can be analyzed.

One piece of advice that students hear a lot is to present a well-rounded profile. High school students are often instructed by their parents and counselors to pursue a sport, a club, a volunteering activity, and maybe an instrument. This is a pretty good strategy for most universities, and college admissions officers certainly notice this type of profile. Well-rounded applications like these are sometimes called a *circle*, a term that some private admissions counselors use.

The opposite type of student is someone who presents a more lopsided profile. This person typically has a single strong passion or pursuit and has focused on that activity, sometimes to the detriment of other parts of life. Competitive figure skaters or ballet dancers often present themselves this way, and so do top-level young physicists or computer scientists. Admissions counselors sometimes call these applicants *angles*, because of the sharp, prominent nature of the singular talent they possess.

While the angular applicants tend to get accepted by highly selective schools, the circular students are much more numerous. In high school, it's not easy to leap from one to the other, especially becoming an angular student, which requires several years of dedication. Still, both paths are good in life, and you should pursue whichever one is most natural for you.

It is also worth thinking about extracurricular activities in light of different criteria. Look at the extracurricular activities pursued by the following two hypothetical students and see if you can identify the difference in their personalities.

- **Student A**: Five years of club soccer, lead tenor in school choir, president of Model United Nations
- **Student B**: Member of golf team, piano lessons at private studio, won a math competition unconnected to school

Can you spot the difference? Student A prefers being in groups, while Student B prefers individual pursuits. It's also likely that Student A is an extrovert, and it's equally likely that Student B is an introvert. Admission committees notice things like this. They may have orders to admit more group-oriented students in order to increase social participation in campus events, and give the nod to Student A. Or they may feel that their school needs more people who march to the beat of their own drummer, and admit Student B instead.

It's worth thinking about these things.

Here's another hypothetical pair of students. See if you can spot the differences in their personalities, based on extracurriculars only.

- **Student A**: Joined robotics club, won an internship at a laboratory, earned a black belt in taekwondo
- **Student B**: Founded a mental health counseling group at school, published a book of original poetry, started a clothing business via Instagram

The difference: Student A joined pre-existing organizations and excelled in them, while Student B invented new activities that hadn't existed before. It's easier to join a group that someone else formed, so if you haven't dreamed up at least one thing that didn't exist yet, it might be worth doing so, especially if you've got your sights set on a highly selective school.

Try to view yourself as a product that's being marketed to a potential buyer. This is a turnaround from the frightened way that many high school students go about the process, but fear won't get you very far in the application process, nor in life. It's much better to view each school as a potential lead, and you decide which leads are the "hottest" ones. Take control, as much as possible!

In the process, you should try to formulate a hook that you will use to sell yourself. Try writing it down and run it by some friends and family to see how it sounds. This should take out any egotism and fear from the process.

Let me show you what I'm talking about. Look at these brief applicant profiles:

- **Student A**: point guard and captain of varsity basketball team, student body vice president, member of DJ club
- **Student B**: volunteer at teen mental health hotline, CPR certification from Red Cross, member of future medical professional club

- **Student C**: chess club, taught himself how to use an Arduino board, enjoys Sudoku

Can you summarize each of these students in a single phrase or sentence? Use this structure:

This student is a _____ *who likes to* _____.

Student A: This student is a *quick-thinking extrovert* who likes to *organize people*. Point guards need to make the quickest decisions on a basketball court, and likewise DJs have to always be preparing the next track to bring into the mix. A student body vice president is most likely an extrovert who promises new forms of organization.

Student B: This student is a *sympathetic helper* who likes to *fix people*. Anybody who listens to strangers' problems on the phone must have a lot of empathy. That, plus the CPR certification, indicates that she likes to heal people, either mentally or physically. The future medical professional club underlines these observations.

Student C: This student is a *systematic thinker* who likes to *work within well-defined parameters*. Chess features a strict set of rules and guidelines, and while it does permit innovation within those limits, a person who pursues this game generally feels most comfortable within a pre-existing system. Sudoku is an even more restrictive pastime, with no improvisation permitted at all to achieve the solution. An Arduino board, which reads inputs and transforms them into outputs, appeals to the same type of systematic mind. This person is almost certainly going to study engineering.

Defining yourself in this way can help reduce stress during the application process and further sharpen the types of college experiences that will be right for you. Furthermore, college admission representatives almost certainly use this type of shorthand when discussing applicants, so it's useful to think the way that they do.

Finally, we do have a metric that tells us exactly how important each aspect of an application is to colleges and universities in general. In 2023, NACAC (National Association for College Admission Counseling) conducted a survey asking four-year colleges to rate the aspects of undergraduate applications that they considered most strongly when making their decisions.

The results shouldn't be very surprising, since they mirror much of the advice in this book. Nearly 77 percent of the schools placed "considerable importance" upon the *grades earned in college prep courses*, such as AP classes or honors classes. Over 74 percent of the schools placed the same considerable importance upon *total high school grades*, and nearly 64 percent upon the *strength of high school curriculum*.

There were many other categories listed, but nothing else came close to those numbers under considerable importance.

Again, let me repeat the three clear winners:

-grades earned in college prep courses
-total high school grades
-strength of high school curriculum

Note that all of them are academically related.

Under the column marked "moderate importance", the only categories that broke 40 percent were *extracurricular activities* and *letters of recommendation*.

Under the column marked "no importance", about 30 percent of schools reported being uninterested in *admission test scores (SAT/ACT)* and *high school class rank*. Almost 55 percent placed zero importance upon the *interview*, and—surprisingly—about 50 percent reported no interest in *AP exam scores*. This could be because those schools are more interested in student performance in the AP class overall, not only the exam.

Admissions representatives will also review the profile of your high school as part of the overall application review process. The reason for this is to level the playing field, since not all high schools are built equally.

If you've never seen one, a high school profile lists the programs available (or not) to students at that school, such as Advanced Placement, International Baccalaureate, Honors offerings, and Dual Enrollment courses, just to name a few. These offerings vary from school to school, and in some cases restrictions are placed on students, such as the number of Advanced Placement courses they are permitted to enroll in. The admissions representatives become familiar with the school profiles from each of the high schools within their territories. This gives them a better understanding of how applicants challenged themselves, based on the programs available to them. They particularly look for whether or not the students built ramps for themselves by taking advantage of all the offerings at their high schools.

It doesn't mean that you had to take college level courses as a freshman, but admissions representatives will certainly look to what extent you challenged yourself, compared with other students at your high school. They can do this because many high school profiles offer grade distributions that provide the college admissions representatives a comprehensive look at how you performed compared with your peers.

If you are a college-bound student, you should familiarize yourself with your high school's profile because it provides detailed information about your school's curriculum and the courses available to you. It will help give context in terms of how much you challenged yourself based on what was available to you. On my podcast, college admissions representatives consistently spoke about wanting to see that students challenged themselves with rigorous courses at some point through high school, based on what was available. Being familiar with your high school's offerings can help you demonstrate on your application how you engaged based on what was available to you.

CHAPTER 22
THE THINGS THAT ARE OUT OF YOUR HANDS

UP UNTIL NOW, one thing has driven this book: the assumption that the power to earn acceptance to a college or university lies in the hands of the applicant. I do feel strongly that we are the captains of our own fate, and that there are many things that a high school student can do to maximize the likelihood of being accepted to a college or university.

That said, there are some things that you have no control over. This chapter will address some of those things.

Colleges and universities do exist to educate their undergraduates, but that is only one of their many purposes. Some schools chase after grant money and outside sources of research funding, particularly in STEM fields. Some schools exist as prestigious brand names, and over time the protection of that brand becomes their most important mission. Other schools focus on training graduate students and demanding professors to publish many academic papers. Other schools want to prepare students for basic employment and make money while doing it. And a few schools exist because they are so old and so well known that they cannot be allowed to fail.

My point is that your needs as an applicant are not the same as the needs of the institution. When an applicant is rejected from a school, it is often (but not always) unrelated to weaknesses in the application.

If that happens to you, remember this: *the school has its own admissions agenda*. We like to believe that a university admissions office is fair and equitable in all instances, or that it acts like a blank slate, with no history and no preferences in anything. We like to imagine the admissions office gazing across a whole landscape of applicants, plucking out only the purest and most qualified, and placing them gently on a champion's podium.

But that's not true.

The fact is that those admissions offices are under a lot of pressure from the highest levels of their administrations to form a particular type of freshman class. As Jeff Selingo, higher education author and journalist (Episode 204), said, "We tend to think admissions is about the seniors applying to college. But it has everything to do with the college and university, and not very much to do with the students at all. It is very much a process driven by the priorities of the colleges and universities, and their priorities are delivered through the admissions office, whether they want more full payers, or they want more kids from a certain geographic part of the country. They might need a third baseman for the baseball team. Things like that."

So admissions offices are active and some would say even ruthless in sifting through the crowd of applicants every year in order to find the select individuals who fit certain niches on campus. They have set up several buckets in advance, and they decide which bucket the applicant gets tossed into, if any.

The external factors that can affect your chances of admission include **legacy admissions**, **quotas**, **athletics and performing arts**, **yield rates**, and **family income**.

Let's look at each of those in some detail.

———

LEGACY ADMISSIONS

By far, this is the most important non-controllable aspect of your application. Many colleges and universities reserve a certain number of seats in every freshman class for the sons or daughters of alumni.

These accepted applicants—the children of older graduates—are called *legacy admissions*.

Before discussing that, let me head off topic, just for a brief moment, into something closely related. It's needed to give background.

For those of us who are a bit older, race-based affirmative action has been the biggest attention-grabber in college admissions. This policy started way back in 1978, when the Supreme Court ruled that colleges and universities could consider race in college admissions when attempting to create a diverse class of incoming freshmen. This has been the policy for most of our lives, and the chief complaints about it came from the families of certain applicants who felt that their chances of winning admission were reduced as their children were being passed over in favor of less qualified minorities. These complaints, and the reactions to them, grabbed the majority of the news headlines for decades, because racial topics often cause outrage in the United States, and writing or speaking about them guarantees a larger set of eyeballs.

But that all changed in June 2023, when the U.S. Supreme Court struck down the use of affirmative action in college admissions. Suddenly, for the first time in 45 years, U.S. colleges and universities were prohibited from considering the race of the candidate in their admissions decisions. The aftershocks of this decision are just starting to be felt. Harvard did release some demographic data on the class of 2028—the first one admitted without considering race—and while the racial makeup of their class didn't change, the percent of applicants who declined to identify their race increased from 4 percent to 8 percent. Certainly, other data will be released in coming months and years.

But the important takeaway here is this: race used to be a way that schools could legally craft their own classes to a predetermined shape or look. But now that lever has been removed.

What remains is *legacy admissions*, and it has taken affirmative action's place as the new villain working against meritocracy.

That is not an undeserved reputation. Legacy admissions were initially founded by Ivy League schools in the 1920s as a way to prevent Jewish students from gaining access to their privilege, and to keep their population purely Protestant. Some of the anti-Semitic things that the presidents of Yale and Harvard publicly said back then are nearly unprintable today.

Those attitudes were slowly phased out, but legacy admissions remained. Today, legacy status is a powerful but mostly invisible way that colleges and universities create an unequal playing field. Many insiders—people who actually work in this sector of education, such as high school counselors—often consider legacy admissions to be the real higher education privilege, not race or anything else. In other words, this is where schools quietly tip the scales in favor of certain applicants, and because they are usually not obligated to reveal any of that information, you will most likely never know about it.

In fact, legacy admissions can be seen as a counterbalance to affirmative action. Whereas affirmative action tried to expand the access to higher education, legacy admissions seeks to continue limiting that access to families who are already literally grandfathered into the system. Democratic Rep. Alexandra Ocasio-Cortez (NY-14) has famously referred to legacy admissions as "affirmative action for the privileged".

From a marketing standpoint, it is understandable why colleges and universities give preference to the children of their previous alumni. They're building brand loyalty. If a young person knows that his grandfather and father both went to a certain university, and if they've dragged him to that university's football or basketball games for most of his young life, there is likely a strong pressure in that family for the young grandson to follow in his family's footsteps. And he very well may give in to that pressure. Plus, those families tend to grow wealthier as time passes, which results in the families donating more money to the schools.

On the other hand, critics often say that this system keeps the silver spoon of wealth and privilege continuing to feed the mouths of the children of the families who need that help the least. College admissions officials rarely discuss legacy admissions in public the way they've spoken publicly about affirmative action, despite the fact that only one-third of all admissions directors at private schools believe that legacy status is an appropriate thing to consider when making admissions decisions.

In the end, a university is no different from any other company offering a product. And companies love repeat customers. You could even view the legacy admissions system as a type of loyalty rewards program. The families who were lucky enough to get into those loyalty rewards programs early were able to take advantage of networks of prestigious social connections, which yielded economic advantages as the decades rolled on. This has created what is now called generational wealth.

So, who considers legacy admissions in their review process?

The 2018 Survey of College and University Admissions Directors was conducted by *Inside Higher Ed* in collaboration with Gallup. It revealed that 42 percent of private schools have a legacy admissions policy, while only 6 percent of public universities do so. This makes sense, since private schools are primarily dependent upon tuition money, while public schools subsist partly on tax money.

In some cases, public state universities have ended their legacy programs. In 1996, after the state of California banned affirmative action in their public education policies, the University of California voluntarily chose to put a stop to all legacy admissions policies. Other public schools have been forced to do so by their state legislatures. In 2021, Colorado became the first state to outright ban legacy admissions in its public colleges and universities. In 2024, Virginia and Maryland have chosen to do the same. Most recently, in September 2024, Governor Gavin Newsom of California signed a complete ban of all legacy admissions in his state, in both private and public schools. In 2022, nearly 15 percent of the freshman class at USC (the University of Southern California) had come from legacy admissions, and Stanford had selected nearly 14 percent in the same year.

Still, public schools acknowledge legacy status in other ways, primarily through dedicated scholarships targeted towards legacy students. Many other schools, from the University of Washington to MIT to Caltech, never indulged in legacy admissions to begin with.

Overall, private schools are fonder of legacy admissions. While more than 100 private schools have abolished legacy admissions since 2015, they are nonetheless still popular at highly selective schools with acceptance rates of less than 25 percent. In recent years, Dartmouth and Yale each admitted about 11 percent of their freshman class from legacy applicants, while Stanford and Cornell were slightly higher, with 15 percent. And Harvard leads the pack with over 30 percent of its students being legacies.

Think about that. One out of three students at Harvard had a parent who also graduated from Harvard.

This sometimes causes resentment and contempt from the great crowds of families around the U.S. with dreams of Ivy League acceptances dancing in their eyes. This might also explain why 75 percent of all Americans oppose the consideration of legacy status in admissions, according to a 2022 Pew Research survey. More significantly, 92 percent of all college admissions directors favor eliminating it.

In fact, the left has been calling for decades to totally end the practice, but the sad truth is that the system will favor applicants from wealthier families regardless. Privileged students are more likely to be offered and to take advantage of educational opportunities that make them attractive to colleges. Privileged students are often socially more comfortable in the hallways of higher education, since their parents typically are from this socioeconomic class, and they know how to conduct themselves in that type of environment without even thinking about it. You can find many accounts of first-generation college students arriving at elite private colleges and universities and struggling to overcome the cultural and social gaps they encounter. Former First Lady Michelle Obama was a first-generation college student, and she has spoken and written about this experience when she attended Princeton University in the nineteen-eighties. Eliminating legacy admissions could chip away at a very entrenched privileged class, but it will not suddenly create a utopian state of pure equality.

QUOTAS

While limits on the number of students of a specific race or gender are a thing of the past, colleges and universities still freely use other types of quotas.

- **U.S. regions**. As mentioned previously, you will have better luck applying to a school far from home if that school is lacking students from your region. Some colleges set themselves the explicit goal of expanding their reach beyond the 200-mile radius that they are accustomed to receiving applications from. Likewise, the opposite can happen, as a school tries to define itself as more local, though this is less common.
- **International Students**. Many schools place a firm cap on the number of international students that they will offer acceptance to, as discussed in previous chapters. Within that capped number, a school can place caps upon acceptances from certain regions of the world or even upon individual countries. However, these decisions are often made informally around the decision table, at the end of the process, rather than stated in advance, as an admissions committee attempts to shape its freshman class.

ATHLETICS AND PERFORMING ARTS

These two categories are more similar than you may think, since both involve public spectacles put on by students who are generally unpaid.

To universities, athletes are more valuable than artists, for the simple reason that they bring in a lot more money. The Big Ten athletics conference, for example, was responsible for $880 million dollars in revenue in 2023. For better or for worse, wealthy alumni are more likely to open their wallets for a winning football team than a winning flute soloist in the orchestra. In fact, some have compared athletics to the front porch of a college. Sports are often the first thing that a typical person encounters about a school, and so it's the first way that the person forms an opinion of that school.

For this reason, a certain number of seats are reserved for athletes at most schools. At many highly selective schools, academically high achieving athletes are more unusual in the applicant pool than academically high achieving performing artists, so they are pursued heavily.

At the same time, for students in the performing arts, a strong supplementary portfolio can really move the needle and open doors to acceptances by certain schools that might be less interested in the same applicant if he or she had applied in a different major. A young actor who goes on to become a prestigious stage or screen actor can reflect very well upon the university that found her, and bring some good attention, so schools do keep an eye out for that type of talent too.

The point is that both of these groups have their own buckets. And a certain number of them are guaranteed seats in a freshman class, which limits the space available for everybody else.

YIELD RATES

It's been mentioned before in this book, but yield rates refers to the percent of students who enroll in a college or university after having been offered admission.

First, look at what Rick Clark, Assistant Vice Provost & Executive Director of Admission at Georgia Tech (Episode 200), said about institutional priorities. "Every college, no matter how big or small they are, starts with one very key driver for their institutional priority, and it is called class size. That is institutional priority number one. Chapel Hill is going to have a class size goal and they are going to get a certain number of applications for those spots, and based on their historical yield, that's going to dictate their admit rate."

Schools use predicted yield rates, based on previous years' data, to guarantee themselves tuition revenue. If a school offers admission to 100 students, and 70 accept, that means the yield rate is 70 percent. This is necessary information for those schools to fill all available seats.

The more prestigious the school, the higher the yield rate. Despite that, you may be surprised to know that even the most glamorous schools don't achieve a perfect 100 percent yield. For the class of 2027, MIT's yield was 86 percent, and Harvard's yield was 84 percent.

Yes, that means that approximately 15 of every 100 students offered admission at MIT and Harvard turned those schools down.

Also for the class of 2027, Duke's yield was 60 percent, and Johns Hopkins's yield was only 48 percent. That means that a majority of the students offered admission at Johns Hopkins turned the school down.

Meanwhile, all four of those schools had admission rates in the single digits. So try to picture this system from a bird's eye view. The most prestigious schools in higher education reject almost everybody who applies. Meanwhile, of those who are offered admission, some (or many) turn down the schools.

Does that make you see the college admissions game differently? It should. There are many applicants turning down some of the biggest names in the game.

You probably haven't looked at it from the point of view of the university, but every year schools spend a lot of time and money estimating exactly how many of these students will do that. After all, their operating budgets depend on the accuracy of this guess.

And make no mistake about it, this is an estimation. Schools are throwing darts at a board, attempting to predict the future yield based on previous yields. Some of them even hire expensive data firms to analyze the data for them, since protecting and maintaining their yield numbers are so valuable, both financially and reputationally.

The covid-19 pandemic really shook up the yield numbers. During that time, colleges discovered the financial challenges that come from suddenly lower yield results, which emphasized the importance of yield protection. After the end of the pandemic, however, application numbers skyrocketed, which made it harder for schools to predict enrollment numbers, because they were using pre-pandemic data.

Another external factor affecting yield rates is the shift away from mandatory standardized testing. As most of the nation went test-optional, schools found themselves inundated with a wider, more diverse pool of applicants than ever before, specifically students who in the past had felt locked out of applying to a certain level of university because of their low test scores. Now that test scores were optional, many decided to roll the dice, and admissions offices were flooded with a new group of applicants whose behavior was unpredictable because the schools didn't have good data about those types of student profiles. This has greatly impacted predicted yields.

For all these reasons, Early Decision has become quite popular with certain schools. After all, it removes the uncertainty of the yield. It also positively affects national rankings, because high yield rates and low acceptance rates indicate selectivity.

The cycle goes like this: When a school accepts a higher percentage of ED applicants, word gets out that the school is now offering an advantage, a secret backdoor entrance to that school. Then that school will likely see a larger number of ED applicants the next year, and the year after that, etc. This will create a virtuous circle of applicants, almost like a self-fulfilling prophecy. That school will have built for itself a large pool of fully committed students to draw from each year. This also offers students a solid application strategy. Washington University in St. Louis states on its website that "[e]ach year we bring in about 55-60% of our class through our early rounds", with a 27 percent acceptance rate from early decision alone. Emory accepted 32 percent of its ED applicants for the class of 2028.

Who is the loser in this scenario? Most the students who apply regular decision. When a university picks a huge portion of its freshman class by December 1, all the people who are planning to send in their applications in January are competing for an ever-shrinking number of seats.

FAMILY INCOME

The typical applicant has zero control over his or her family's income, but that simple string of numbers can impact admissions. The amount by which it impacts admissibility varies depending on the school. It's a complex dance between finances, scholarships, and financial aid.

To be specific, there are need-blind and need-aware schools. The difference between the two is simple: need-blind schools do not consider family income when making their decisions, and need-aware schools do. It is certainly possible that need-aware schools do favor students whose families can demonstrate the ability to pay full tuition. I wouldn't let this stop you from applying to need-aware schools, but be sure to apply to need-blind schools as well.

CHAPTER 23
FINANCIAL AID - HOW TO AFFORD COLLEGE

THERE IS SO much to say about financial aid that I could write an entire separate book about it. In fact, many people have done exactly that. There are hundreds of books on the topic.

Here's a quick overview: College is expensive, so most families have to get some help. Different schools offer different types of financial aid. Some only offer what is called *need-based aid*, which considers your family's financial situation. Other schools offer *merit aid*, which is awarded based on academic performance in high school.

After you apply for financial aid, the package that you receive often consists of loans, which you have to pay back, and grants or scholarships, which you do not have to pay back.

Financial aid definitely seems overwhelming at first, but if you take the time to study what aid you're eligible for at different schools, that time spent will pay off very well in the long run.

The skyrocketing price of college is one of the most-talked-about stories of higher education in the last few decades. In fact, the average cost of tuition has more than tripled in the last half century.

You may reply: *Well, that doesn't mean anything, inflation has increased the cost of everything in the last half century.*

Unfortunately, that statistic *does* include inflation. So let's look at that with numbers. The actual cost of college has tripled in the last half century, from $4648 in 1964 to $14,307 in 2021 (all measured in adjusted 2021 dollars). The biggest increase during this time was seen from 2001 to 2021—roughly the last twenty years—when the average cost of tuition leaped from $8661 to $14,307 (again, all measured in adjusted 2021 dollars).

For a middle-class family, the squeeze is real. The smart play is to have invested early—ideally, at the birth of the child—for the money to compound over the next eighteen years. But not everyone has had the ability to make that happen, for many different reasons.

One problem is that colleges, like health insurance companies, have not done a good job in communicating the actual cost of college to prospective applicants. This may be done by accident or by design, but either way, the people are owed more transparency in the process.

At the very least, there is a federal mandate for colleges and universities to make available their net price calculators to students and their families on their websites. This is part of the Higher Education Opportunity Act (HEOA) of 2008 whose purpose was to provide more transparency in the cost of attending college while providing a good estimate of available financial aid. The U.S. Department of Education has a College Scorecard, which provides a comprehensive overview of schools throughout the United States including cost, graduation data and so much more.

Schools offer financial aid, but this faucet doesn't spew an endless amount of money, and colleges and universities have to decide if a student has financial need and how much they're going to award them. This need is based on the student's family's finances.

To assist them in making this decision, schools use something called FAFSA, one of the better-known acronyms in the world of higher education. It stands for Free Application for Federal Student

Aid. Nearly 20 million U.S. families fill out this form each year. In 2024, the FAFSA currently consists of only 36 questions (down from 108 questions in the past!), and much of the data needed can be taken directly from a family's federal income tax return on file with the IRS. In other words, it's been simplified and streamlined.

It's also more popular than ever. Over 87 percent of all undergraduate applicants receive financial aid in some way, and the average loan is about $7500 per year. By contrast, in the year 2000, only about 70 percent of all undergraduate applicants received financial aid.

The federal government uses the FAFSA to calculate a number called Student Aid Index (SAI). This number calculates how much you can possibly afford for one year of college education, therefore determining whether or not you are eligible for a Pell Grant and the government's lowest-cost loans. The SAI formula uses income, assets, the number of persons in the household, and the number of those attending college for the award year.

College financial aid officers often use your SAI number to help them put together a group of grants, scholarships, work-study programs, and loans that they intend to offer you to entice you to come to their school. This should, ideally, make it financially possible for you to attend their school.

The SAI formula is tweaked periodically. In 2022, families with an adjusted gross income of $60,000 or less, and who have filed a simple tax return, began to have their SAI calculated with no assets included, which is good news for them. In fact, the trend has been towards qualifying more lower-income students for Pell Grants: in 2024, over 600,000 more students have qualified for Pell Grants as a result of changes to the SAI. At the same time, upper-middle-class families have found their SAI number climbing higher, which reduces access to loans. Most significantly, the sibling discount was removed in 2024, which will affect large families the most, since each applicant is considered individually and not as part of a collective group of brothers and sisters.

Affording college is a difficult situation, and the very worst place to be is squarely in the middle class. The majority of middle-class families earn incomes that are too high to qualify for Pell Grants, need-based scholarships, or other significant types of financial aid. At the same time, those same middle-class incomes don't come close to covering the high out-of-pocket costs of college. If they haven't been saving for a very long time, those families are forced to rely upon loans with high interest rates. The data backs this up too. The families with household incomes of $80,000 to $90,000 end up with the most student debt as a proportion of their incomes.

Another organization, the College Board (which hosts the SAT), offers a totally different financial aid application called CSS (College Scholarship Service) Profile. Filling out the CSS Profile is required by about 250 private colleges and universities (and some independent scholarship programs) to award non-federal financial aid. Many of the most prestigious schools in the United States use the CSS, so if you're shooting for Stanford or something like it, please complete it.

Unlike FAFSA, the CSS Profile is not free: it costs $25 to select the first university or scholarship program, and then $16 for each additional one. It also asks for more information than FAFSA does, such as family home ownership. But the financial aid available through CSS is often worth far more than the limited Pell Grant money available through FAFSA, which is capped at $7395 per year. And unlike FAFSA, a student only needs to fill out a CSS Profile once, instead of doing yearly renewals. In fact, you are permitted to change it only one time during college.

Schools do offer information regarding financial aid and scholarships, so do not be shy about asking admissions representatives about expenses, including room and board, tuition, and books. Those are additional costs, in addition to tuition, and you want to get a complete picture of the entire cost before making decisions.

What happens if the financial aid package offered by a college isn't quite what you were hoping for? One thing to do is to try to negotiate. Through email, nicely let the admissions committee know that you have received the offer of a better financial aid package elsewhere, and be ready to show proof. It also helps if the applicant is near the top of their pool, meaning they want you to attend badly. It's possible that they could make a better counteroffer. Some people are stricken by fear at the thought of communicating with a college admissions committee, but don't think twice about driving a hard bargain with automobile salespeople. The two aren't that different. You can avoid paying sticker price for both cars and college tuition.

The financial aid game has been accused of being rigged. In fact, in July 2024, Dartmouth and 16 other universities agreed to pay a $166 million settlement proposal in a class-action lawsuit against them for violating antitrust laws and conspiring to minimize financial aid for ordinary working families. The lawsuit alleged that the universities simply favored applicants from wealthier families, and found ways to limit the aid they could promise needy students. Six other top universities had earlier agreed to a similar $118 million settlement proposal in two separate lawsuits. If everything gets approved by a federal judge, it will be a total of $284 million in settlement money. That is a large amount of cash, and the attention that these lawsuits have received will probably open up this area for more analysis in coming years.

Jeff Selingo, higher education journalist and author (Episode 204), agrees that something smells fishy in the world of financial aid. He explained, "Colleges are either need *blind* or need *aware*. There's a lot of colleges that are need *blind* in the admissions process, meaning they don't take an applicant's financial background into consideration. But it doesn't mean that they're necessarily generous with financial aid. While some colleges are need blind and meet full demonstrated need, those are very few colleges that have a lot of money. But other colleges that are need-blind tend to *gap* students."

I asked him what that meant, and he continued.

"In other words, students demonstrate they need a certain amount of money, and colleges meet them halfway, but they don't give them all the money that they need. Then there's a group of colleges that are need aware, and those colleges basically say, we *could* be need blind, but we don't have enough money to give to everybody. So we are actually going to be need *aware*, meaning we are going to look at your financial background in admissions. And if we feel like we can't give you the money you need, if we just don't have enough to go around, we are going to deny you. That's because we think ethically it's better to deny you than to accept you, but not give you enough money to come here. There's a big debate in admissions over this."

One final note: be sure to know the difference between a direct *subsidized* loan and a direct *unsubsidized* loan.

First, their similarities. Both subsidized and unsubsidized loans are federal student loans provided by the Department of Education. For eligibility, both require you to be enrolled in school at least part-time. And both nicely offer a six-month introductory period before you're required to begin repayment.

The major difference between the two types of loans relates to the interest owed. For a direct *subsidized* loan, you won't be charged interest while you're enrolled in school or during your six-month introductory period. However, for a direct *unsubsidized* loan, the interest starts accruing from the date of your first loan disbursement (a fancy word for the day you receive the funds from your school).

The way interest accumulates is the greatest difference between these two types of loans, but there is another smaller difference too: the total amount of money you're allowed to borrow. There's a limit on each loan's dollar amount, and that number depends upon your year in school as well as your student status, particularly whether you're a dependent or independent student.

Your school will decide which loan type you qualify for. Your school will also tell you the amount you can borrow based on your financial need, your cost of attendance, and other financial aid you might have received.

CHAPTER 24
A WORD ABOUT TWO-YEAR COLLEGES

BE true to who you are as a student. The simple fact is that not everyone goes to college, and not everybody attends a four-year school from the beginning. In fact, many students start at a two-year school, then transfer to a four-year school later.

One benefit of this: it is an excellent way to save money, and it is thus a favorite of many people who benefit from an extensive and well-equipped community college system in their states. This exact point has come up in more than a few episodes, and I even did an interview with Orange Coast College (Episode 115). Currently, the average yearly tuition at a two-year college is $3,862, while the average in-state tuition at a four-year public university is $9,377. Community colleges also feature smaller class sizes than introductory classes at four-year public universities do, which means more individual attention for students. An easier application process (no SAT or ACT) plus flexible class schedules round out the advantages of this path.

There are plenty of people taking advantage of this system of schools. In fall 2021, there were 4.7 million students enrolled at two-year institutions, a bit less than half the 10.8 million students enrolled at four-year institutions. The big difference between the two is that 65 percent of the students at two-year institutions were only attending part-time, as compared with 27 percent of the students at four-year institutions. This reflects the reality that many students have financial, medical, or familial pressures that prevent them from pursuing full-time college.

Some students hesitate to select a community college path because they worry it could impact their resumes. The fact is that most careers value the final degree—a bachelor's degree—more than where or how you earned it.

This topic resonates with me on a personal level because I started my college journey at a two-year school, SUNY Delhi. After one year, I transferred to SUNY Stony Brook, where I completed my degree. Since then, I've been fortunate to continue my education, earn a doctoral degree in School Administration and Supervision, serve as a high school principal in one of the best schools in the country, and host a podcast on college admissions. My experience has shown me that it's less about how you begin and more about the path you create for yourself.

CHAPTER 25
FINAL ADVICE

LET me end this book with three bits of advice.

- **Academic excellence.** The closest thing we have to a golden ticket in college admissions is the pursuit of knowledge. Be sure that you are always trying to learn something that interests you. That passion will shine through the application and be recognized by admissions committee members.
- **Authenticity.** When you identify what you love to do, or what type of person you are, and then discuss these things openly in your application, good things tend to result. This is as true in life as it is in college admissions. We humans tend to notice people who are unusually frank, honest, and self-aware. It's a valuable trait. In the words of Jason McGrath, director of undergraduate admissions at UNC-Chapel Hill (Episode 199): "Don't try to package yourself in a way that you think is what we want. You telling your story is what we want to hear. If you try to sound like what you think we are looking for, if you start to package yourself in those ways, you'll start to sound like a lot of other applicants, as opposed to being authentically yourself. And

at least if you know you put your authentic self as an applicant forward, you would never have any regrets when the process is done. Because if we don't find in you what you hope we will, then you shouldn't come here anyway. Right? Because you deserve to go somewhere that finds the values in what you offer and sees the good fit, so you will thrive."

- **Build a narrative**. Connected to authenticity is the idea of building a story to describe yourself in your application. Construct a narrative through-line that is simple, clear, and memorable. I already discussed this in a previous chapter, but it is important enough that it bears repeating. Pretend that your life is a Pixar movie, and you as the main character. What is your purpose? What is the conflict that prevents you from achieving that purpose? How have you overcome previous obstacles? What is your greatest strength? Asking yourself these types of questions is the first step on the road to success.

Keep in mind that applications are, in general, thinner than they've ever been. Standardized tests are no longer mandatory everywhere, consideration of race has been made illegal, and legacy admissions are dwindling. This means that what's left for college admission representatives to consider about your packages includes your grades, your activities, and your personal statement and essays. (Many schools also still use letters of recommendation but weigh them less than other elements.)

For this reason, it's more crucial than ever that you take the reins and tell them your story. Don't duck your head, pretend to be invisible, and hope that someone will see your talent. Don't assume anything. There are many adults who can help you to be noticed.

In the end, most of us should end up where we belong. This is because college admissions isn't a race to be won, it's a match to be made. Following the advice in this book will help you make that match.

As Iva Bory, assistant director of admissions at Syracuse University

(Episode 109) stated, "Even if you're not admitted to ten different colleges, you are going to be admitted where you belong. You're going to be admitted to the school that has looked at your credentials and has determined that this is where you are going to be successful."

Finally, if you're in high school, there are certain patterns that those four years often follow. Below is a list of things that you could do, or expect to encounter, each year. Preparing yourself for each of these scenarios will maximize your chance of admission at the school of your dreams.

9th grade. This is a great year to sample many different clubs, sports, or organizations. The purpose is to find two or three that you really enjoy, and stick with them! If you already have activities from middle school that you enjoy, continue with them as well. There is almost nothing that admissions committees respect more than a high school student with persistence and commitment.

Some schools, such as the University of California system, do not officially enter ninth grade classes into their internal calculation of your GPA, but that doesn't mean you get a free pass. As Jua Howard, assistant director of admissions at University of California-Berkeley (Episode 206), said, "Just because the ninth grade is not factored into the calculation does not mean we are not looking at your freshman year grades. Because I am."

10th grade. This is the time for you to amp up your dedication to your extracurricular activities. You may find yourself in your first leadership role. You may suggest new events or methods of marketing and find that others actually take you seriously, unlike most ninth graders. Academically, this is the year when most students take their first AP classes, so if you have one in mind, don't hesitate to sign up. You can always transfer out if it's too difficult.

11th grade. This should be the most difficult academic year of your high school experience. Ambitious students will feel the brunt of two or three or even more AP classes. Honors classes grow plentiful in student schedules. And you're expected to do more even for regular classes. On top of that, many students are now fully committed to extracurricular activities, e.g. taking on leadership roles. To complicate things further, this is the school year when students get their first driver's licenses, which is even more classwork, studying, and exams. Try to stay focused and balanced.

During this year, some students try to also prepare for standardized tests such as the SAT, if it is a necessary part of their application packages. If you can handle that extra work on top of your schoolwork, then go for it. However, for some students, this could be taking on too much responsibility, as they are often burdened with academic work to pay full attention to an exam in the distant future. Burnout is a real possibility. Remember that eleventh grade tends to sharpen everybody's academic skills, and the results will be evident in the exam that autumn.

12th grade. The first semester will feel like you're standing in a wind tunnel. If you're like most people, you'll probably have the heaviest course load of your academic life, same as junior year. You'll have senior status in all your extracurricular activities, which saddles you with extra work. And, on top of it all, the college application process is going to demand so much of your time that it alone could be considered a part-time job. In short, you won't sleep much. Smart, organized students will use July and August to write their personal statements, finalize their college lists, and begin researching their answers to the supplementary essays.

The second semester, however, is totally different. The college applications have been submitted, and seniors begin to feel a certain relaxation setting in. These are the early warning signs of the dreaded senioritis. By April, as colleges and universities begin responding to regular decision applications, this affliction grows even more deadly.

The one warning I will offer is this: many colleges and universities reserve the right to reject you in June—even after you've accepted their offer of admission—if your second semester senior year grades fall by more than one letter in any class. So take heed! As Jua Howard, assistant director of admissions at University of California-Berkeley (Episode 206), said, "For twelfth grade, even though we don't have your grades yet, we are still looking at the rigor of your courses, because we're expecting you to continue a level of excellence. So twelfth grade needs to be strong. You have to finish strong."

As you reach the end of this book, remember that the resources I have provided don't end here. By continuing to listen to *The College Admissions Process Podcast*, you'll stay updated with the latest insights, advice, and real conversations with college admissions representatives from across the country and beyond. Use the alphabetical list of colleges featured on my website as your personal, on-demand virtual college fair that can help you explore a variety of schools that might be the right fit for you.

Scan the QR code below to access the alphabetical list of podcast episodes available.

Whether you're just starting out with your college search or are in the middle of completing your applications, these resources are here to support and guide you. This book is only the beginning. If you stay connected with *The College Admissions Process Podcast*, you'll always have the most up-to-date information to help you navigate the process with confidence.

I wish you all the best and continued success on your journey. Thank you for letting me be part of it!

JOIN MY EMAIL LIST

Scan this QR code to stay updated with more insights and resources!

ADDITIONAL RESOURCES

The Federal Student Aid Handbook. https://fsapartners.ed.gov/knowledge-center/fsa-handbook/2024-2025

The National Association for College Admissions Counseling (NACAC). The college fairs in particular are worth looking at. https://www.nacacnet.org/

The National Center for Education Statistics. https://nces.ed.gov/

U.S. Department of Education College Scorecard. https://collegescorecard.ed.gov/

Hamilton College - Essays That Worked. https://www.hamilton.edu/admission/apply/college-essays-that-worked

Johns Hopkins University - Essays That Worked. https://apply.jhu.edu/college-planning-guide/essays-that-worked/

Macalester College Workshop Wednesdays. https://www.macalester.edu/admissions/workshop-wednesdays/

Colleges That Change Lives. https://ctcl.org/

Net Price Calculator. There is no single site that provides a net cost for every school in the U.S., but you can search for school-specific net price calculators. This link can provide further information. https://collegecost.ed.gov/net-price

Common Data Set. Most colleges publish their CDS on their official websites, offering great insights into enrollment, graduation rates, number of students admitted, rejected, waitlisted, and so much more. To find it, search "Common Data Set" along with the name of the school you're interested in.

The National Association of Student Financial Aid Administrators provides some very good state-specific financial aid advice. www.savingforcollege.com www.nasfaa.org/State_Financial_Aid_Programs

Student Aid Index Calculator. https://www.mefa.org/student-aid-index-sai-calculator

Scholarship Search Tool. https://www.careeronestop.org/toolkit/training/find-scholarships.aspx

Filling out the FAFSA. https://studentaid.gov/apply-for-aid/fafsa/filling-out

Khan Academy, the official test preparation partner for the College Board. https://www.khanacademy.org/

Free, full-length practice tests on the College Board website. https://satsuite.collegeboard.org/practice/practice-tests

Free ACT Test Prep & Resources. https://www.act.org/content/act/en/products-and-services/the-act/test-preparation/free-act-test-prep.html

The Chosen: The Hidden History of Admission and Exclusion at Harvard, Yale, and Princeton, by Jerome Karabel.

Great website to help find scholarships:
https://studentaid.gov/understand-aid/types/scholarships

How Much Will College Cost?:
https://bigfuture.collegeboard.org/pay-for-college/get-started

Mefa College Cost Calculator: https://www.mefa.org/college-cost-calculator

PODCAST EPISODES

Below is a list of the first 250 episodes of the College Admissions Process Podcast. Because multiple new episodes are being added weekly, you should follow the QR code at the end of this chapter for a fully up-to-date list of episodes.

1. Adelphi University - Jade Ean-Heller - Asst. Director of Admissions
2. High Point University - Nikki Short - Admissions Counselor
3. The Ohio State University - Lauren Heatherly - NY/NJ Regional Recruitment Manager
4. Syracuse University - Part 1 - Asma Malik - Director of Admissions, Metropolitan NY Office
5. Syracuse University - Part 2 - Asma Malik - Director of Admissions, Metropolitan NY Office
6. SUNY Geneseo - Suzanne Miller - Admissions Counselor
7. Michigan State University - Larry Alterman - Manager of East Coast Recruitment
8. Bucknell University - Josh Wilkinson - Associate Director of Admissions for Communications
9. Penn State University - Laurie Wax - NY Metro Regional Admissions Counselor
10. Sacred Heart University - Pamela Pillo - Executive Director of Admissions
11. University of Florida - Jessica Roth - Assistant Director for Scholarships and Regional Recruitment
12. University of Michigan - Hailie Smith - Recruitment Coordinator
13. Iona College - Benny Rivera - Admissions Counselor and liaison to the Honors Program
14. Cornell University - Ian Schachner - Sr. Associate Director
15. SUNY Oswego - Kate Anderson - Assistant Director of Admissions
16. Boston College - Amy Chung - Senior Assistant Director
17. University of Delaware - Matt Lucatamo - Admissions Counselor
18. Muhlenberg College - Eric Thompson - Associate Director of Admissions and Coordinator of Transfer Admissions
19. University of Arizona - Joseph Elliott - Sr. Associate Director, Undergraduate Recruitment
20. Fairfield University - Christopher Cahill - Associate Director of Undergraduate
21. Susquehanna University - Gloria Darko - Admissions Representative
22. University at Albany - Danielle Haft - Admissions Counselor
23. Hobart and William Smith Colleges - Ryan Hofmann - Asst. Director of Admissions
24. University of South Carolina - Kate Henchy - Admissions Representative
25. Drew University - Meghan Walsh - Assistant Dean of Enrollment Management
26. Vanderbilt University - Briana Grimes - Admissions Counselor
27. University of Georgia - Kelly Coffman Bird - Senior Assistant Director
28. NYU - Arianna Yarritu - Senior Assistant Director of Admissions

182 PODCAST EPISODES

29. Student Athlete Series - Episode 1 - Lacrosse Coach John Calabria
30. Student Athlete Series - Episode 2 - Lafayette College - Camryn Monfort, Division I Women's Soccer Player
31. Student Athlete Series - Episode 3 - Yale University - Jack Monfort, Men's Lacrosse Player
32. Student Athlete Series - Episode 4 - Northwestern University - Kendall Halpern, Division I Women's Lacrosse Player
33. Tulane University - Bailey Gabrish - Senior Admissions Counselor
34. Stony Brook University - Robert Pertusati - Associate Dean of Admissions
35. Manhattan College - Nick Marter - Associate Director of Admissions
36. University of Miami - Charles M. Cammack - Associate Director of Undergraduate Admissions & Kaitlyn Marshall - Admissions Counselor
37. Student Athlete Series - Episode 5 - St. John's University - Aidan Borra, Division I Men's Soccer Player
38. Georgia Tech - Samantha Rose-Sinclair - Assistant Director of Admission & Digital Media
39. St. John's University - Lisa Sayo - Senior Assistant Director of Admissions
40. Wake Forest University - Morgan Wehrkamp - Assistant Dean of Undergraduate
41. Student Artists with Taylor Pacis - Stamps School of Art and Design at the University of Michigan
42. The Cooper Union - Hillary Fernandes - Associate Director of Admissions
43. George Mason University - Josh Price - Admissions Counselor
44. University of Colorado Boulder - Clark Brigger - Executive Director of Admissions
45. Indiana University - Brandi Samaroo - Senior Assistant Director of Admissions
46. University of Kentucky - Cara Franke - Director of Undergraduate Recruitment
47. Carnegie Mellon University - Ben Carpenter - Senior Assistant Director of Admissions
48. Marist College - Kelli Nienstadt - Assistant Director of Admissions
49. James Madison University - Joanna Caples - Admissions Counselor
50. Panel Discussion with Admissions Counselors
51. University of Tampa - Alexandra Landry - Assistant Director of Admissions
52. University of Rhode Island - Brianna Montecalvo - Admission Advisor
53. University of Connecticut - Bryan Feener - Admissions Counselor
54. Ithaca College - Jessica Kowalewski Dietrich - Associate Director for Regional Recruitment
55. University of Pittsburgh - Dr. Lauren Olivia Wright - Director of Undergraduate Recruitment
56. Hunter College, CUNY - Jarvis M. Dieujuste - Admissions Counselor
57. SUNY Cortland - Alex Contento - Admissions Advisor
58. Common App - Suzanne Miller (SUNY Geneseo) & Kate Anderson (SUNY Oswego)
59. Providence College - Michael Splann - Admissions Counselor
60. Temple University - Michael Usino - Assistant Dean of Admissions, Enrollment Management & Student Recruitment
61. Union College - Vernon Castillo - Senior Associate Dean of Admissions
62. Iowa State University - Renee Denofrio - Regional Admissions Counselor

PODCAST EPISODES 183

63. University of Texas at Austin - Sam Torres - Admissions Advisor
64. University of Rochester - Erica Padilla - Regional Associate Director, NY Metro Area
65. Notre Dame - Don Bishop - Retired Associate Vice President for Undergraduate Enrollment
66. Santa Clara University - Becky Konowicz - Dean of Undergraduate Admissions
67. Rochester Institute of Technology - Michael Navarrete - Assistant Director of Undergraduate Admissions
68. Emory University - Tim Fields - Senior Associate Dean
69. Williams College - Lance Ledet - Admissions Counselor
70. Scholarship Help - Special Episode with Monica Matthews
71. University of California - Davis - Leticia V. Garay - Assistant Director of Admissions
72. Miami University - Tyler Margolis - Assistant Director for Regional Enrollment (Northeast)
73. Pomona College - Tina Brooks, Ph.D. - Associate Dean of Admissions
74. Purdue University - Megan Dorton - Senior Associate Director of Admissions
75. University of California - Riverside - Ashley Swengler - International & Out-of-State Admissions Specialist
76. University of Illinois Chicago - Maureen Woods - Director of Undergraduate Admissions
77. Rice University - Tamara Siler - Deputy Director of Admissions
78. Manhattanville College - Troy Cogburn - Vice President for Admissions and Marketing
79. William & Mary - Nina Fortune' - Admissions Counselor
80. New York Institute of Technology - Thomas Shea - Director of Undergraduate Admissions
81. Franklin & Marshall College - Mariah Wagner - Admissions Counselor
82. University of Maryland - Rosemary Martin - Associate Director of Undergraduate Admissions
83. University of Maine - Christopher Richards - Director of Undergraduate Enrollment Management
84. Trinity College - Dayla Whaley - Admissions Counselor
85. Claremont McKenna College - Jennifer Sandoval-Dancs - Associate VP for Admission and Financial Aid
86. Duke University - Christoph Guttentag - Dean of Undergraduate Admissions
87. Loyola Marymount University - Jenelle Abbattista - Assistant Director of Undergraduate Admissions
88. University of Minnesota - Nick Hervatin - Freshman Admissions Counselor
89. University of California, Irvine - Michelle Burns - Senior Admissions Counselor & Regional Recruiter
90. Music and The College Admissions Process with Michael Salzman
91. Carleton College - Adam Webster - Senior Associate Dean & Director of Admissions
92. Georgia Institute of Technology - Rick Clark - AVP & Executive Director of Undergraduate Admission
93. Drexel University - Nicole Kalitsi - Admissions Counselor
94. Wesleyan University - Chandra Joos deKoven - Director of Admissions

184 PODCAST EPISODES

95. Long Island University Post - Thomas Butler - Director of Freshman Admissions
96. Wellesley College - Lauren Kudisch - Associate Director of Admissions
97. Quinnipiac University - Erika Castillo - Associate Director of Admissions
98. Gonzaga University - Rosa Velasco - Admission Counselor
99. Boston University - Pete Saenz - Assistant Director of Admissions
100. Farmingdale State College - Dr. John Nader - President
101. The College of New Jersey - Kristina Fasulo - Admissions Counselor
102. Hamilton College - J.D. Ross - Associate Dean of Admission
103. Colgate University - Rob Israel - Admissions Counselor
104. Some Insights from 100+ College Admissions Reps: Advice for Parents and Students
105. University of California - Santa Barbara - Lisa Przekop - Director of Admissions
106. Virginia Tech - Exree Hipp III - Assistant Director of Undergraduate Admissions
107. Southern Methodist University - Brenda Del Rio - Admissions Counselor
108. Grinnell College - Conner Stanfield - Senior Admission Counselor
109. Syracuse University - Inside the Admissions Office: Expert Insights, Tips, and Advice - Iva Bory - Assistant Director of Admissions
110. Rhode Island School of Design (RISD) - Inside the Admissions Office: Expert Insights, Tips, and Advice - Michael Cameron - Director of Admissions
111. San Diego State University - Inside the Admissions Office: Expert Insights, Tips, and Advice - Danielle Toglia - Regional Admissions & Recruitment Manager
112. Clemson University - Inside the Admissions Office: Expert Insights, Tips, and Advice - Dr. Rick Barth - Director of Undergraduate Admissions
113. Emerson College - Inside the Admissions Office: Expert Insights, Tips, and Advice - Rebecca Schmaeling - Senior Assistant Director of Undergraduate Admissions
114. DePaul University - Inside the Admissions Office: Expert Insights, Tips, and Advice - Noah Fogarty - Assistant Director of Undergraduate Admission
115. Orange Coast College - Inside the Admissions Office: Expert Insights, Tips, and Advice - Kristoffer Toribio - Manager of International Admissions & President of the International Association for College Admissions Counseling
116. University of Alabama - Inside the Admissions Office: Expert Insights, Tips, and Advice - AnnaMae Lang - Regional Recruiter
117. University of Denver - Inside the Admissions Office: Expert Insights, Tips, and Advice - Todd Rinehart - Vice Chancellor for Enrollment
118. University of Illinois - Urbana-Champaign - Inside the Admissions Office: Expert Insights, Tips, and Advice - Dr. Andy Borst - Director of Undergraduate Admissions
119. University of San Francisco - Inside the Admissions Office: Expert Insights, Tips, and Advice - Jonathan Rice - Director of Admissions
120. Auburn University - Inside the Admissions Office: Expert Insights, Tips, and Advice - Billy Fisher - Manager, Freshman Recruitment - Undergraduate Admissions
121. Ringling College of Art and Design - Inside the Admissions Office: Expert Insights, Tips, and Advice - Kirche Zeile - Northeast Regional Admissions Counselor
122. Arizona State University - Inside the Admissions Office: Expert Insights, Tips, and Advice - Brad Baertsch - Senior Director of Admissions
123. Bowdoin College - Inside the Admissions Office: Expert Insights, Tips, and Advice - Emily Almas - Director of Admissions

PODCAST EPISODES   185

124. Revolutionizing Dorm Room Decor: Amanda Zuckerman, Co-Founder of Dormify - Shares her Inspiring Journey
125. Rhodes College - Inside the Admissions Office: Expert Insights, Tips, and Advice - Lauren Sefton - Director of International Admission
126. College of Mount Saint Vincent - Inside the Admissions Office: Expert Insights, Tips, and Advice - Andrew Curiel - Director of the Center for Leadership
127. Cornell University - Inside the Admissions Office: Expert Insights, Tips, and Advice - Playback Wednesdays - Ian Schachner - Sr. Associate Director
128. American University - Inside the Admissions Office: Expert Insights, Tips, and Advice - Kevin Medina - Director, Special Populations & Transfers
129. University of Michigan - Inside the Admissions Office: Expert Insights, Tips, and Advice - Playback Wednesdays - Hailie Smith - Recruitment Coordinator
130. Insights from "The College Admissions Process Podcast": Interview with Mike Bergin & Amy Seeley
131. - Duke University - Inside the Admissions Office: Expert Insights, Tips, and Advice - Playback Wednesdays - Christoph Guttentag - Dean of Undergraduate Admissions
132. Pace University - Inside the Admissions Office: Expert Insights, Tips, and Advice - Danielle Fusaro - Admissions Counselor
133. University of California - Santa Barbara - Inside the Admissions Office: Expert Insights, Tips, and Advice - Playback Wednesdays - Lisa Przekop - Director of Admissions
134. Scripps College - Inside the Admissions Office: Expert Insights, Tips, and Advice - Lyanne Dominguez - Associate Director of Admission Diversity and Access Initiatives
135. Rick Clark & The Truth About College Admission - Inside the Admissions Office: Expert Insights, Tips, and Advice - Playback Wednesdays
136. Keuka College - Inside the Admissions Office: Expert Insights, Tips, and Advice - Erica Doherty - Director of Undergraduate Admissions
137. Carnegie Mellon - Playback Wednesdays - Inside the Admissions Office: Expert Insights, Tips, and Advice - Ben Carpenter - Senior Assistant Director of Admissions
138. Binghamton University - Inside the Admissions Office: Expert Insights, Tips, and Advice - State University of New York - Douglas J. Harrington - Assistant Director of Undergraduate Admissions
139. University of Texas at Austin - Inside the Admissions Office: Expert Insights, Tips, and Advice - Playback Wednesdays
140. Reflections about "The College Admissions Process Podcast": Interview with Sam from the Financial Samurai Podcast
141. Mastering Standardized Tests with Prep Expert: Insider Secrets from Shaan Patel, Prep Expert CEO
142. Common Application Overview - Inside the Admissions Office: Expert Insights, Tips, and Advice - Playback Wednesdays
143. College Essay Help Straight from the Admissions Office
144. Purdue University - Inside the Admissions Office: Expert Insights, Tips, and Advice - Playback Wednesdays
145. Tips for Aspiring Nursing Students - Special Episode - Temple University

146. NYU - Inside the Admissions Office: Expert Insights, Tips, and Advice - Playback Wednesdays
147. Bryn Mawr College - Inside the Admissions Office - Nichole Reynolds - Dean of Undergraduate Admissions
148. Pomona College - Inside the Admissions Office: Expert Insights, Tips, and Advice - Playback Wednesdays
149. Occidental College - Robin Hamilton - Sr. Associate Dean of Admission, Director of Recruitment & Equity
150. Emory University - Inside the Admissions Office: Expert Insights, Tips, and Advice - Playback Wednesdays
151. Colleges That Change Lives - Ann Marano - Executive Director
152. Wagner College - Anthony Rinaldi - Assistant Director of Admissions
153. Boston University - Inside the Admissions Office: Expert Insights, Tips, and Advice - Playback Wednesdays
154. University of California - Panel Discussion Straight from the Admissions Offices
155. University of Wisconsin-Madison - Inside the Admissions Office: Expert Insights, Tips, and Advice - Andre E. Phillips - Director of Admissions and Recruitment
156. Claremont Colleges - Panel Discussion - Inside the Admissions Office: Expert Insights, Tips, and Advice
157. University of Tennessee - Inside the Admissions Office: Expert Insights, Tips, and Advice - Sheryl Tingling - Regional Admissions Representative
158. Loyola Maryland University- Inside the Admissions Office: Expert Insights, Tips, and Advice - Joann Wang - Assistant Director of Regional Recruitment
159. Glion & Les Roches - Inside the Admissions Office: Expert Insights, Tips, and Advice - Riana Pizzi - Admissions Representative
160. Siena College - Inside the Admissions Office: Expert Insights, Tips, and Advice - Anthony Pelliccia - Associate Director of Admissions & Athletic Department Recruitment
161. Seton Hall University - Inside the Admissions Office: Expert Insights, Tips, and Advice - Katherine Fainer - Director of Admissions
162. Le Moyne College - Inside the Admissions Office: Expert Insights, Tips, and Advice - Dr. Timothy Lee - Vice President for Enrollment Management
163. University of New Hampshire - Inside the Admissions Office: Expert Insights, Tips, and Advice - Mahmoud Sowe - Senior Assistant Director of Admissions
164. Florida Gulf Coast University - Inside the Admissions Office: Expert Insights, Tips, and Advice - Yasmin Galindo - Admissions Counselor
165. Columbia University School of General Studies (GS) - Inside the Admissions Office: Expert Insights, Tips, and Advice - Matthew Rotstein - Director of Admissions
166. University of Pennsylvania - Sara Cohen, Associate Dean & Barkley Barton, Associate Dean for Evaluation & Selection
167. University of California - San Diego - Inside the Admissions Office: Expert Insights, Tips, and Advice - Pamela Franco - Admissions Officer
168. Worcester Polytechnic Institute - Inside the Admissions Office: Expert Insights, Tips, and Advice - Sydney Trahan - Admissions Counselor
169. Sacred Heart University - Follow-Up Episode - Pamela Pillo - Asst. VP of Undergraduate Admissions

170. Johns Hopkins University - Inside the Admissions Office: Expert Insights, Tips, and Advice - Patrick Salmon - Associate Director of Recruitment
171. Test Prep Help - Revisiting our Conversation with Shaan Patel, Prep Expert
172. Mississippi State University - Inside the Admissions Office: Expert Insights, Tips, and Advice - Grant Nerren - Assistant Director of Recruitment
173. University of Oregon - Inside the Admissions Office: Expert Insights, Tips, and Advice - Joelle Rankins Goodwin - Senior Associate Director for Recruitment & Outreach
174. Northwood University - Dr. Matthew L. Bennett - Vice President of Graduate Enrollment and Professional Studies
175. Nova Southeastern University - Brooke Stevens - Director of Undergraduate Admissions
176. Florida Atlantic University - Inside the Admissions Office: Expert Insights, Tips, and Advice - Mary Gately - Admissions Counselor
177. Colorado State University - Inside the Admissions Office: Expert Insights, Tips, and Advice - Sam Whitaker - Admissions Counselor
178. Louisiana State University (LSU) - Julian Radney - Associate Director in Enrollment Management and Student Success
179. University of Iowa - Chris O'Sullivan - Assistant Director of Admissions
180. Robert Franek - Editor in Chief - The Princeton Review
181. University of Kentucky - Lewis Honors College - Dean Christian Brady
182. Agnes Scott College - Inside the Admissions Office: Expert Insights, Tips, and Advice - Emily-Davis Hamre - Associate Director of Admission
183. Lynn University - Inside the Admissions Office: Expert Insights, Tips, and Advice - Justin Wentzel - Senior Asst. Director of Admission
184. Washington State University - Inside the Admissions Office: Expert Insights, Tips, and Advice - Andrew Brewick - Director of Admissions
185. St. Louis University - Rachel Adelman - Program Coordinator: West and Southwestern States
186. Mastering the Digital SAT: Exclusive Insights with Shaan Patel, Prep Expert CEO
187. International Schools - Panel Discussion
188. University of Scranton - Hugh J. Doyle Jr. - Director of Undergraduate Admissions
189. Champlain College - Inside the Admissions Office: Expert Insights, Tips, and Advice - Emily Rudolph - Associate Director in the Office of Undergraduate Admissions
190. Macalester College - Inside the Admissions Office: Expert Insights, Tips, and Advice - Elyan Paz - Assistant Vice President & Dean of Admissions
191. Goucher College - Inside the Admissions Office: Expert Insights, Tips, and Advice - Megan Steely - Assistant Director of Admissions for Visitor Engagement
192. Bard College - Inside the Admissions Office: Expert Insights, Tips, and Advice - Tessa Greenhalgh - Admissions Counselor
193. Texas Tech University - Rex Oliver, Director of Recruitment & Jennifer Mauppin, Associate Director of Recruitment
194. Bates College - Audrey Burns - Associate Dean of Admission & Director of Recruitment
195. College of Charleston - Grace E. Vail - Admissions Counselor
196. President of the College of Mount Saint Vincent - Dr. Susan Burns

PODCAST EPISODES

197. Pepperdine University - Inside the Admissions Office - Gianna Mack - Admission Counselor
198. Saint Peter's University - Inside the Admissions Office: Expert Insights, Tips, and Advice - Mason Traino - Senior Assistant Director of Transfers
199. UNC Chapel Hill: Exclusive Insights from Jason McGrath - Associate Provost and Director of Undergraduate Admissions
200. The Truth About College Admission (2nd Edition) with Rick Clark - Author, Assistant Vice Provost & Executive Director of Admission at Georgia Tech
201. Duquesne University - Marisa M. Germinario - Assistant Director of Undergraduate Admissions
202. Villanova University - Erica Woods - Senior Associate Director
203. UCLA - Karly Brockett - Senior Associate Director of Admissions
204 Jeff Selingo - Higher Education Author & Journalist
205. Marquette University - Inside the Admissions Office: Expert Insights, Tips, and Advice - Mario Walker - Admissions Counselor
206. UC Berkeley - Jua Howard - Assistant Director of Admissions
207. Lehigh University - Bruce Bunnick - Director of Admissions
208. Carnegie Mellon University - Gloria A. Darko - Assistant Director of Admission
209. U.S. Merchant Marine Academy - CDR Mike Bedryk - Director of Admissions
210. Transform Your Dorm with Dormify: Exclusive Interview with Co-Founder Amanda Zuckerman and learn about Special Discounts
211. Emory University - Follow-Up Episode - Tim Fields - Sr. Associate Dean of Undergraduate Admission
212. Navigating College Admissions with Tim Fields and Shereem Herndon-Brown, Co-Authors of "The Black Family's Guide to College Admissions"
213. Florida State University - Andrea Flores - Assistant Director of Recruitment
214. Hofstra University - Director of External Relations in the Office of Undergraduate Admissions - Hofstra University
215. High Point University - Katie McKeon - Admissions Counselor
216. University of Cincinnati - Andy Wright (Associate Director for Recruitment & Outreach) & Jen Sloan (Assistant Director for National Recruitment & Outreach)
217. Oberlin College & Conservatory - Manuel Carballo, Vice President & Dean of Admissions & Financial Aid & Tom Abeyta, Director of Admissions
218. Pitzer College - David Girvan - Senior Associate Director of Admission
219. University of California - Panel Discussion - Playback Wednesdays - Straight from the Admissions Offices
220. Elon University - Evan Sprinkle - Dean of Undergraduate Admissions
221. University of Pennsylvania - Playback Wednesdays - Sara Cohen & Barkley Barton
222. St. John's College - Benjamin Baum - Vice President of Enrollment
223. University of Wisconsin-Madison - Playback Wednesdays - Inside the Admissions Office: Expert Insights, Tips, and Advice - Andre E. Phillips - Director of Admissions and Recruitment
224. Rutgers University - New Brunswick Campus with Drew Newitt - Admissions Counselor
225. Johns Hopkins University - Playback Wednesdays - Inside the Admissions Office:

PODCAST EPISODES 189

Expert Insights, Tips, and Advice - Patrick Salmon - Associate Director of Recruitment
226. University of South Carolina - Marissa Strominger - NY/Fairfield County (CT) Regional Admissions Representative
227. The Truth About College Admission (2nd Edition) with Rick Clark - Playback Wednesdays - Author, Assistant Vice Provost & Executive Director of Admission at Georgia Tech.
228 - University of Delaware - Matt Lucatamo - Assistant Director of Admissions
229. UNC Chapel Hill: Playback Wednesdays - Exclusive Insights from Jason McGrath - Associate Provost and Director of Undergraduate Admissions
230. Adelphi University - Jade Frevola - Associate Director of Admissions
231. University of Calgary - Bailey Fawcett - Student Recruitment Advisor
232. UC Berkeley - Playback Wednesdays - Jua Howard - Assistant Director of Admissions
233. Bucknell University - Lara Guerrero Schmitt - Assistant Director of Admissions for Access and Outreach
234. Carnegie Mellon University - Playback Wednesdays - Gloria A. Darko - Assistant Director of Admission
235. Fairfield University - Follow-Up Episode - Christopher Cahill - Associate Director of Undergraduate Admissions
236. Colorado School of Mines - Jen Gagne - Executive Director of Admissions
237. Lehigh University - Playback Wednesdays - Bruce Bunnick - Director of Admissions
238. NACAC Board of Directors Member - Christine Loo - Director of College Counseling at The Stony Brook School, NY
239. Fordham University - Dr. Patricia Peek - Dean of Admission
240. Cornell University - Follow-Up Episode with Ian Schachner - Sr. Associate Director
241. University of Miami - Follow-Up Episode - Charles Cammack, Director of Recruitment & Kaitlyn Marshall, Assistant Director of Admissions
242. Vaughn College - Nick Marter - Assistant Vice President of Admissions
243. Boston College - Inside the Admissions Office: Expert Insights, Tips, and Advice - Amy Chung - Associate Director of Admissions
244. Lafayette College - Dysean Alexander - Assistant Director of Admissions
245. University of Vermont - Christopher Perlongo - Associate Director
246. University of Washington - Alex Hall - Admissions Counselor
247. Rensselaer Polytechnic Institute (RPI) - Jon Wexler - VP of Enrollment
248. Middlebury College - Samuel N. Prouty - Executive Director of Admissions
249. Coastal Carolina University - Trey Wilson - Director of Undergraduate Admissions
250. Brown University & Michigan State University - A Conversation about Similarities and Differences

190   PODCAST EPISODES

Scan this QR code for an updated alphabetical list of podcast episodes available.

ABOUT THE AUTHOR

Dr. John Durante, a proud alumnus of Stony Brook University, has dedicated over 30 years of his life to education, as both a teacher and administrator. Since 2010, he has served as the principal of Syosset High School in Long Island, New York, playing a key role in its recognition as one of the top high schools in the country. Under his leadership, the school has earned numerous accolades for its academic achievements, including being designated a National Blue Ribbon School of Excellence by the U.S. Department of Education in 2016, and its alumni continue to reflect its commitment to excellence. In 2005, he earned a doctoral degree in School Administration and Supervision from St. John's University, and was recognized by his alma mater for his achievements in education.

Dr. Durante launched *The College Admissions Process Podcast* in 2022. With hundreds of episodes, it has become a valuable resource for students, parents, and college counselors around the United States and beyond. His work, both as an educator and podcast host, reflects his unwavering dedication to helping others achieve their full potential.

You can learn more at the College Admissions Process Podcast website: www.collegeadmissionstalk.com

For speaking engagements, interviews, or to share your thoughts, please contact Dr. Durante at: john@collegeadmissionstalk.com

www.ingramcontent.com/pod-product-compliance
Lightning Source LLC
Chambersburg PA
CBHW032043150426
43194CB00006B/404